Reader's Digest
Basic Home
Woodworking
Manual

Reader's Digest
Basic Home Woodworking Manual

**Expert guidance
on woodworking
tasks in the home**

Published by
The Reader's Digest Association Limited
London • New York • Sydney • Montreal

Contents

Tools and techniques

8   The woodworking tool kit
15   Tool maintenance
17   Choosing and buying wood
20   Measuring and marking wood
22   Cutting wood and boards
29   Drilling wood
32   Shaping wood by hand
35   Using a router
37   Nailing
39   Fixing with screws
42   Making joints
48   Smoothing wood
50   Using wood filler
51   Painting woodwork
53   Varnishing woodwork
54   Using waxes and oil finishes

Woodworking projects

Shelving and cupboards

58   Choosing wall fixings
60   Choosing shelving
62   Strengthening shelves with battens and lipping
63   Finding your levels
64   Putting up a fixed shelf
65   Shelves in alcoves
67   Built-in cupboards

Flat-pack furniture

70   Self-assembly fixings for flat-pack furniture
72   Assembling flat-pack furniture
74   Customising flat-pack units
75   Assembling flat-pack shelves
76   Building a computer desk

Walls
78 Wood mouldings
79 Fitting picture rails and dados
81 Removing and replacing skirting boards
84 Preparing to clad a wall with tongue-and-groove panelling
86 Lining a wall with tongue-and-groove panelling

Floors
88 Curing loose and squeaking boards
89 Restoring a wood floor
90 Restoring a woodblock floor
90 Sanding and varnishing a wood floor
92 Laying a wood mosaic floor
94 Laying a laminate floor

Stairs
97 Fixing creaking stairs
98 Repairing broken balusters

Doors and windows
99 Putting up or replacing architraves
100 Curing faults in doors
103 How to hang a front or back door
105 Fitting a letterplate and knocker
106 Replacing broken sash cords
109 Renewing parting beads and staff beads

Furniture restoration
112 Blemishes
114 Repairs
118 Stripping
120 Finishes

125 **Index**
128 **Acknowledgments**

Basic tools and techniques

The woodworking tool kit

These are the tools you will need if you plan to tackle DIY woodworking tasks around the home, from laying laminate flooring and replacing skirting boards to putting up shelves and cupboards. The toolkit includes all the basic DIY tools as well as more specialist woodworking tools.

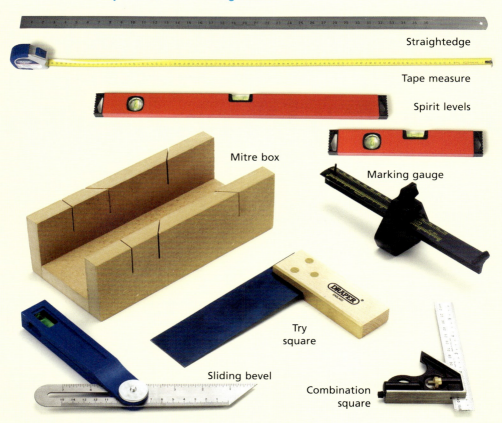

Straightedge

Tape measure

Spirit levels

Mitre box

Marking gauge

Try square

Sliding bevel

Combination square

Tools for marking

Straightedge
A long steel or aluminium straightedge is essential for marking and checking straight lines. Buy one 1m long for maximum usefulness, with both metric and imperial markings along it.

Tape measure
You need a steel tape measure for measuring and estimating jobs. An ideal size is a 5m tape, which will cope with measuring up a room as well as taking smaller measurements. Most have metric and imperial markings, so you can use the tape as a handy conversion device. Pick one with a lock that keeps the blade extended while you use it.

Spirit level
This tool is essential if you are to get items like shelves level, and for checking anything that needs to be truly vertical. It is a plastic or alloy bar with vials containing an air bubble set into the long edge and usually at each end. The level is horizontal or vertical when the bubble is exactly centred between the marks on the appropriate vial. Buy a metal one at least 300mm long. To check levels over longer distances, you can balance it on a timber straightedge.

Mitre box
A three-sided open-ended box with guide slots pre-cut in its opposite sides, used to guide a tenon saw blade when making 45° mitre cuts. The size of the box restricts the size of pieces that can be cut with it.

Marking gauge

This tool consists of a wooden beam with a hardened steel pin set into it near one end, and a wooden block that slides along the beam and can be secured to it with a thumbscrew. The pin scribes a line at a fixed distance from the edge of the workpiece. It is used when marking out woodworking joints, and is also useful for jobs such as centring locks on door edges and marking the depth of hinge recesses.

Try square and combination square

A try square has a rectangular metal blade fixed at 90° to a wooden, metal or plastic stock. It is an essential tool for marking a cutting line at right angles to the edge of a workpiece, and is also used for checking internal and external angles. A combination square is a variation on the theme, with a movable stock that can be used to mark 45° angles as well as right angles.

Sliding bevel

This tool is a sort of adjustable try square with a metal blade that can be set at any angle and locked in place with a wing nut. It is particularly useful for fitting shelves in out-of-square alcoves, and for fitting staircase balusters.

Tools for sawing

Tenon saw

Invest in a tenon saw, which has a rectangular blade about 250mm long stiffened along the top with a strip of brass or steel. The handle is either wood or moulded plastic. As its name implies, the tenon saw is designed primarily for cutting

woodworking joints, but it will cope with all sorts of other minor woodwork jobs such as trimming wall battens or cutting a shelf to length. The thickness it will cut is limited by the depth of the blade.

Coping saw

Designed for making curved cuts in wood and boards, it has a slim replaceable blade mounted in a U-shaped steel frame with a handle at one side. The frame holds the blade in tension, and allows the blade to be rotated to prevent the frame from fouling the edge of the workpiece.

Hole saw

This attachment for a power drill is used to cut holes in wood and boards that are larger than the maximum size of a flat wood bit (around 38mm). The blade is a short length of saw formed into a cylinder and fitted into a blade holder. This carries a pilot drill at its centre which starts the hole and guides the saw blade into the wood. Hole saws are sold in sets of several blades, up to about 75mm in diameter.

Mitre saw

This useful tool consists of a framed saw with a fine-toothed blade mounted on guide bars over a steel base. The guide bars can be rotated to position the saw at any angle between 45° and 90° to the workpiece, which is clamped in place between the blade and

Circular saw

Tenon saw

Coping saw

Panel saw

Jigsaw

Padsaw

Hole saw and blade holder

Hole saw blades

Flat wood
drill bits

Screwdriver
bits for drill

Cordless
drill

Masonry
drill bits

Twist drill
bits

Countersink
drill bit

14.4V

the base while the cut is made. It is more accurate than a mitre box, and can cut wider components.

Padsaw

The padsaw has a short tapered blade fitted into a handle, and is used mainly for cutting holes in the centre of the workpiece, such as a keyhole in a door. You need a starter hole so you can insert the blade and start the cut.

Panel saw

The panel saw has a plain steel blade about 560mm long, typically with around 10 teeth per inch (tpi), fitted to a wooden or plastic handle. As its name implies, it is used mainly for cutting up panels of man-made boards by hand, as a low-cost alternative to using a circular saw. The blade may be PTFE-coated to minimise friction, and the best saws have hard-point teeth that will stay sharp for longer than standard teeth. Fit the blade guard when storing the saw.

Circular saw

A circular saw is essential if you plan to cut up sheets of man-made boards, fit your own kitchen worktops or lay floorboards. A circular saw makes accurate, straight cuts, and its tilting soleplate can be set to allow cuts at any angle between 45° and 90°.

A basic circular saw takes blades 150mm in diameter and has a maximum cutting depth of about 45mm. Larger and more powerful semi-professional models take blades 190mm or 230mm in diameter,

offering cutting depths of 65mm and 80mm respectively at 90° and 45 or 60mm at 45°. Some have a dust extraction facility.

Blades are available for fine cutting, cross cutting and rip cutting wood and man-made boards, and for cutting laminated chipboard kitchen worktops. Check that any blades you buy are compatible with your make of saw.

Jigsaw

A jigsaw is one of the most useful of all power tools. It is primarily designed for cutting wood and man-made boards, but can also cut metal and rigid plastic if the correct type of blade is fitted. It has a relatively short blade that protrudes from the baseplate of the saw, and this cuts on the upstroke. Because of the thinness of the blade, you can make curved cuts with it as well as straight ones, simply by driving the saw blade along a marked cutting line. You can also make cuts away from the edge of the workpiece – to fit a letterbox in a front door, for example, or make a cut-out in a worktop for an inset sink or hob.

Features to look out for when choosing a jigsaw are adequate power (at least 500 watts), variable speed, a dust bag or vacuum cleaner attachment to help to collect dust, and a blade fitting arrangement that does not need tools. Keep a stock of standard wood-cutting blades for general work, and buy specialist blades only when you need them.

Cordless jigsaws are available, and although they are comparatively expensive they are useful if you plan to do a lot of cutting far from a power source.

Tools for drilling

Drill

There are corded and cordless drills and each have their advantages and disadvantages. Cordless drills are more versatile and can be used anywhere without the need for a power supply but they are not as powerful and accurate as mains-powered models, and can be more expensive. However, they do double up as a power screwdriver thanks to their low chuck speed, and their reverse gear allows you to undo screws as well. For more information on corded drills, see page 29.

Cordless drills have a rechargeable battery – sizes range from 9.6V (volts) up to a massive 24V. Choose one that is comfortable and well-balanced to hold, and is not too heavy to handle easily. Keep a spare battery, so that one can be kept fully charged while the other is in use.

Drill bits

Your cordless drill will need a range of drill bits for the various jobs it can do.

Twist drill bits Make small holes in wood, man-made boards and metal. Buy a set of HSS (high-speed steel) drill bits containing sizes up to 10mm, stored in a metal case which will last longer than a plastic one. Carbon steel bits are cheaper than HSS ones, but become blunt more quickly.

Flat wood bits Drill larger holes in wood and boards, and come in sizes from 12mm up to 32mm. Buy them as and when you need them and store them in their packaging – usually a plastic sleeve.

Masonry drill bits Make holes in solid walls, usually to take wallplugs when making wall fixings. Do not buy a boxed set, which will contain sizes you will never use. Instead, match the sizes you buy to the wallplugs and other fixings you usually use – probably 6, 7 and 8mm.

Screwdriver bits enable you to drive and remove screws using your cordless drill as a power screwdriver. One two-ended bit will probably be supplied with your drill; add a set containing bits for slotted-head, Phillips, Pozidriv and Torx screws.

Lastly, you will also need a countersink drill bit. This makes cone-shaped recesses in wood or metal to accept the heads of countersunk screws.

Tools for fixing

Hammers

The most versatile hammer to have is a claw hammer, which will drive all but the smallest pins and can also be used to lever out old nails by fitting the grooved claw under the nail head. Choose one with a metal or glass-fibre shaft and a rubber grip, with a head weighing 16 or 20oz (hammers still come in imperial sizes).

To accompany your claw hammer, buy a nail punch (also known as a nail set). This is a small steel tool about 100mm long, with a knurled shaft and a tapered point. It is used with a hammer to drive nail heads below the wood surface, preventing the hammer head from striking and denting it.

Add a small pin or ball-pein hammer to your tool kit if you drive a lot of small nails and panel pins. These are lightweight hammers and have wooden handles.

Ball-pein hammer

Claw hammer

Pincers

Screwdriver set: flat-tip, Phillips and Pozidriv in various sizes

Power planer

Router

Mallet

Surform planerfile

Smoothing plane

Block plane

Honing guide and oilstone

Chisels

Rasp

Screwdrivers

Within reason, you can never have too many screwdrivers. Screws come with head recesses of different types, ranging from straight slots to cross and hexagon shapes, and in different sizes.

To start with, you need a flat-tip screwdriver with a blade about 125mm long for slotted-head screws, and a No. 2 Phillips cross-tip screwdriver which will also drive other types of cross-head screws such as Pozidriv and Prodrive.

If you need more screwdrivers, it is worth looking out for screwdriver sets sold in a storage case. These typically include two or three drivers for slotted-head screws, plus Phillips and Pozidriv drivers in two sizes for large and small cross-head screws of different types. The set may have a master handle, into which you slot the blade you need for the task. This type of set saves space but can be fiddly to use if you have a complicated project in hand.

Pincers

Looking more like an instrument of torture than a DIY tool, pincers are extremely useful jacks of all trades. They are designed primarily for pulling out unwanted pins, tacks and nails – from floorboards, for example – but can also be put to other tasks, such as pulling out picture hooks without damaging the plaster, or nibbling awkward shapes out of ceramic tiles. Pincers are usually about 200mm long, and are inexpensive to buy.

Tools for shaping

Chisels

Chisels are essential for cutting many woodworking joints. They also chop out slots (mortises) for door locks, form recesses for hinges and do all sorts of general paring and shaping jobs. To start with, buy a set of bevel-edge chisels in 6, 12, 19 and 25mm sizes, ideally contained in a storage case so they do not get muddled up with other tools in your tool box. Keep the plastic blade guards on their tips when they are not in use. To keep the blades sharp, you will need an oilstone and some light machine oil. A honing guide will help you to sharpen them at the correct angle.

Mallet

This wooden hammer with a square beechwood head is used mainly for striking chisel handles when cutting woodworking joints, and for assembling joint components.

Planes and power planers

The bench plane is the traditional tool for reducing wood to the cross-sectional size you want, and for finishing it with flat, smooth edges. It consists of a steel blade held at an angle to the tool's soleplate in an adjustable mount. The small block plane and the larger smoothing plane are most widely used.

The power planer does the work of a bench plane much more quickly. It has a rotating cylinder into which a replaceable cutting blade is fitted, and can be used to

Sander

remove up to 2–3mm of wood in each pass of the tool. It can also cut rebates when fitted with a detachable guide, and the groove in its soleplate allows it to chamfer edges too.

Router

The router is a power tool with a motor that drives a cutter at very high speed. Straight cutters produce slots and grooves; shaped cutters create a wide range of edge mouldings. The tool is mounted on a baseplate on springs, allowing it to be 'plunged' into the work to a pre-set depth. Edge and circle guides allow the tool to follow the shape of the workpiece or to cut circular recesses. Many routers now feature dust extraction, and come with a few router bits. Extra bits can be bought singly or in sets as required.

Rasp

This tool is a coarse file used for shaping wood, especially curved surfaces. Buy a half-round rasp with one flat and one curved surface, which will shape convex and concave curves.

Surforms

The Surform range of shaping tools all have perforated blades that work like a miniature cheese grater, removing wood in a series of fine shavings. The range includes planes and files in several styles; the planerfile with its reversible handle is the most versatile. The blades are all replaceable when blunt.

Honing guide and oilstone

This wheeled guide holds a chisel or plane blade at the correct angle while it is being sharpened on an oilstone. It also holds it square to the surface of the stone. The oilstone is made of natural or synthetic abrasive material and usually has a fine and a coarse face; it is lubricated with light machine oil.

Tools for finishing

Sander

Jobs such as restoring old floorboards or finishing new wood require sanding using an abrasive paper to create a smooth surface. You can do the job by hand, but for all but the smallest areas this is one of the most tedious and time-consuming DIY jobs. A power sander does all the work in a fraction of the time, and even gathers up the dust if you buy the right type.

Power sanders come in more varieties than any other tool, ranging from tiny hand-sized finishing sanders to high-powered belt sanders. There are even sanders with interchangeable heads for sanding awkward areas. As a first choice for general smoothing work, an eccentric or random-orbit sander is probably the best. This combines the fine finish of an orbital sander with the fast stock removal of a disc sander, and can be fitted with a wide range of abrasive sheets.

Most random-orbit sanders take circular sanding discs 115 or 125mm in diameter. You attach the discs to the baseplate with touch-and-close (Velcro) fastenings. Holes in the discs line up with holes in the baseplate through which the sander's motor extracts dust, either depositing it in a small dust bag or delivering it via a hose connection to a vacuum cleaner.

Adjustable spanners

Tools for holding and gripping

Spanners

Spanners are better at turning nuts and bolts than pliers. An medium-sized adjustable spanner has a jaw opening up to about 30mm – big enough to cope with most bolts and nuts. The so-called crescent pattern with its offset head is best at getting into awkward positions.

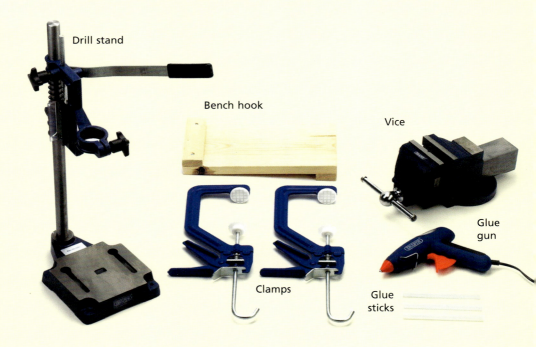

Drill stand

Bench hook

Vice

Glue gun

Clamps

Glue sticks

Workbench tools

Bench hook

This simple wooden bench aid is used to hold small workpieces on the workbench, for example when cutting them to length with a tenon saw (see page 9). The hook is positioned on the workbench with the lower batten against its front edge. The workpiece is held against the upper batten.

Clamps

Clamps come in many different styles and sizes, and are used for two main jobs. The first is holding workpieces securely on the workbench while they are cut, drilled or shaped. The second is clamping components such as woodworking joints together while the adhesive sets. G-clamps and screw clamps are traditional designs, but fast-action trigger clamps and spring clamps are quicker and easier to use.

Drill stand

This bench aid clamps your power drill in an upright position on your workbench, making it easy to drill holes in workpieces at precisely 90° to the work surface – something that is difficult to judge accurately by eye. The running drill is moved up and down in the stand with a lever, and the depth of drilling can be pre-set to create stopped holes if required. Take your drill with you when buying a stand, so

you can check that it will fit. You can also get a dowelling jig which allows you to drill correctly aligned holes for the three most common dowel sizes (6, 8 and 10mm).

Glue gun

This mains-powered tool dispenses blobs of hot-melt adhesive at the squeeze of a trigger, and is invaluable when assembling woodworking joints. The adhesive comes in sticks which you insert into the back of the gun. They are melted and extruded from the nozzle when you squeeze the trigger.

Vice

You can grip large workpieces in the jaws of your portable workbench. However, for smaller items it is useful to have a bench-mounted vice, which you can attach to the workbench as needed. Traditional metal workshop vices are clamped in place; you can also buy a lightweight resin vice that fits into the holes in your workbench jaws.

Workbench

The last essential tool for the home woodworker is a portable workbench. You can use it to support wood while you cut or drill, and its jaws will act as a large vice for gripping the wood. Small basic types are suprisingly cheap; larger models cost more, but may have extra features, such as dual height settings and moveable jaws.

Tool maintenance

Chisel and plane blades must be kept sharp if they are to cut well – and safely. A blunt tool is more likely to slip, injuring you or damaging the workpiece.

Sharpening blades

To sharpen blades you will need an oilstone, a honing guide and some light machine oil. Never use vegetable oil on an oilstone to sharpen tool blades. The mixture of oil and ground-off metal particles will gum up the stone and create a slippery surface glaze so that the stone is no longer abrasive.

When you have finished using the oilstone, rub some sawdust from a non-resinous wood across the stone to clean it. If an oilstone is clogged with oil, soak it overnight in a tin of paraffin or petrol.

Buy a carborundum (silicon carbide) combination oilstone for good all-round performance. It has coarse or medium grit on one side and fine grit on the other. The coarse face removes metal quickly and sharpens tools such as shears, while the fine face puts a cutting edge on chisel and plane blades. The standard size for an oilstone is 200 x 50 x 25mm, but smaller sizes are also available.

Before you start Prepare a new oilstone for use by pouring a teaspoonful of oil onto it and smearing it over the stone. Leave it to soak in, then apply a second spoonful and repeat the process. Wipe off excess oil with absorbent paper.

1 Clamp the blade in the honing guide, following the instructions. Check that the blade projects by the correct distance and tighten the clamping nuts fully.

2 Pour a little oil on the stone (use the fine side if it has two different faces). Move the guide up and down the stone in a figure of eight pattern so you use as much of the surface as possible. You will wear a groove in the stone if you simply run the blade up and down the middle. Press down on the honing guide to keep the chisel tip flat against the stone.

Alternatively If you don't have a honing guide, pour on some oil and place the honed edge on the stone with the blade at an angle of about 45° to it. Reduce the blade angle gradually until a fine line of oil can just be seen welling up along the honed edge of the blade. Hold that angle as closely as you can while you move the blade up and down the stone to sharpen it.

3 Release the blade from the guide. The action of honing a chisel or plane blade on an oilstone produces a thin curl of metal (the burr) on the back of the blade. Take this off by holding the blade absolutely flat on the stone, bevel side up. Then rub its flat side back and forth across the stone until the back is mirror smooth.

4 Hold the blade against the light when you think it is sharp. A really keen edge won't reflect the light, but if you see a fine white line of reflected light, the blade needs more work to bring it to a really sharp edge.

HELPFUL TIPS

• Give a sharpened blade the final touch by stropping it on a piece of leather glued to a softwood offcut (above). Draw the blade bevel side down across the leather, then turn it over, lay it flat and rub it back and forth a couple of times. Don't be tempted to use the palm of your hand as a strop; you risk cutting yourself.

• If you're working away from your bench and don't have an oilstone, make one by sticking a piece of fine silicon carbide paper to a wood offcut.

• Tap a few panel pins into the bottom of an oilstone box, making sure they don't penetrate the stone compartment. Nip off the heads with pincers to leave the ends slightly protruding. These will grip any surface and stop the box sliding about when you're using the stone.

Using a bench grinder

A bench grinder is the quickest and easiest way to sharpen a plane blade if you have access to one. Practise on an old tool to accustom yourself to using a bench grinder. Aim to make light, rapid passes across the wheel, taking off a tiny amount of metal at each pass. Don't apply too much pressure or let the wheel play on one spot; otherwise the blade will overheat, turn blue and be spoilt.

Re-sharpening drill bits

Buy a sharpener for restoring the edge to twist-drill bits. You will soon recoup the expense in the money you will save by not having to replace blunt bits. Most are powered by an electric drill.

Store drill bits upright in a block of wood to prevent them from being damaged. For a perfect fit, drill each hole with the bit to be kept in it.

Restoring a plane

An old neglected wooden plane with cracks in its body can often be restored to make an excellent tool. The blade is usually made of top-quality steel and a wooden sole slides more easily than a metal one over wood. Stop up the throat with putty, then pour linseed oil into it. Over the space of a few days the trapped oil will soak through the wood and the cracks will close up.

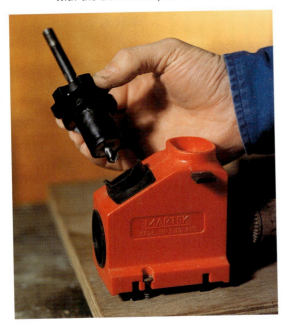

STORE TOOLS SAFELY

Keep drill bits, saw blades, rotary files and other cutting attachments sharp, by removing them from the tool and storing them in suitable containers when you've finished using them. Alternatively, make sure that they are out of harm's way before setting the tool down; raise the blades of a power planer and the cutter of a router.

Choosing and buying wood

The basic raw materials for most DIY woodworking projects are softwood – cut from coniferous trees such as pine and spruce – and man-made boards. Hardwood from deciduous trees such as oak, beech, teak and mahogany is expensive and harder to work than softwood, and is used mainly for making furniture. However, hardwood mouldings are widely available, and are popular because they hold detail better than the softwood equivalent.

Softwood

Softwood is not only easy to work with, but it almost invariably comes from renewable sources, so is not depleting valuable stocks of rare woods or destroying forests.

Buying softwood

You can buy softwood from DIY stores or from local timber merchants. Wood from timber merchants is generally cheaper, and they are much more welcoming to the do-it-yourselfer than they used to be. They also stock a wider range of wood types and sizes.

However, for small amounts of wood, the convenience of the DIY store probably outweighs the extra cost involved.

Softwood sizes

Softwood is available in sawn and planed finishes, in a range of cross-sections that are described in millimetres but are still commonly referred to by their imperial equivalents – 2 x 1in equals 50 x 25mm, for example.

It is important to realise that the quoted sizes are the actual dimensions of the wood when it leaves the sawmill. A piece of sawn wood described as 100 x 50mm will be that size, give or take a millimetre or so to allow for shrinkage. Planing the rough-sawn wood removes from 3mm to 6mm from each dimension, so a piece of planed wood described as 100 x 50mm (its nominal size) will actually measure about 95 x 47mm in cross-section. To avoid mistakes when you are building things in wood, get into the habit of using the measured size of your wood to work out dimensions, rather than the nominal size.

Commonly available widths for softwood are 25, 38, 50, 75, 100, 150 and 225mm (the last usually available only in Parana pine). Common thicknesses are 12, 19, 25, 38 and 50mm.

Softwood is sold in lengths that are multiples of 300mm (known as a metric foot, and about 5mm shorter than the old imperial one). Commonly available lengths are 1.8, 2.4 and 3m.

Structural timbers such as floor joists are available in longer lengths.

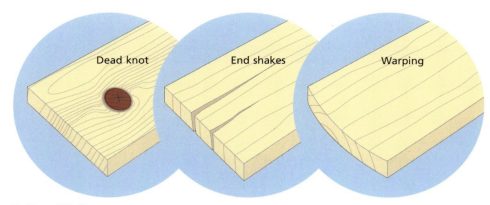

Dead knot — End shakes — Warping

Softwood faults

When buying softwood, check it for faults (see above). The most serious is warping, where the wood is bent or twisted along its length.

This can be disguised when wood is sold in bundles, as in many DIY stores. Do not be afraid to open bundles and examine individual lengths before you buy, because warped wood is useless for most projects. Try to hold the timber at eye level, and look along its length to check for warping. It helps to have someone with you, to hold the other end.

Other faults that can spoil softwood are excessive knots – especially dead ones where the heart of the knot has fallen out – and end splits (called shakes). Reject any wood with these faults because you will find you cannot use it when you get it home.

Hardwood

Hardwood is used in the home mainly in the form of decorative mouldings and as veneers on man-made boards. If you want a particular hardwood as an alternative to softwood – for shelves or a windowsill, for example – look for a specialist timber merchant in your local *Yellow Pages*.

Man-made boards

Man-made boards allow you to use wood wider than that available from any tree. There are two main types: boards made from real wood, glued together in thin veneers or solid strips, and boards made from ground-up wood chips or fibres bonded together into a uniform sheet. Each has its advantages and disadvantages.

Buying man-made boards

Boards of all types are available from DIY stores and timber merchants. As with softwood, timber merchants are generally cheaper and stock a wider range of types and board sizes.

The standard board size for all types is 2440 x 1220mm, a straightforward conversion from the old imperial 8 x 4ft sheet. Most board types are also available in smaller sizes, equal to one half or one quarter of a full-sized sheet (nominally 2440 x 610mm and 1220 x 610mm), and also in 1830 x 610mm panels.

So-called furniture panels – mainly plastic-faced or veneered chipboard (see opposite) intended for shelving and making kitchen cabinets – are now made in metric sizes which are fractionally smaller than their imperial-based equivalents.

Real wood boards

The oldest of the man-made boards is plywood. Blockboard is little used today, its place in the woodworker's stockroom taken by timberboard (also known as stripwood).

Plywood Sheets that consist of a number of thin wood veneers called plies, bonded together with adhesive. The grain direction in each layer is at right angles to that of its neighbours, resulting in a board that is stable and equally strong in either direction. The grain direction of the outer plies (there is always an odd number) runs the length of the board.

The board surface is smooth, but the edges tend to splinter when cut and can be difficult to finish neatly.

Exterior-grade (WBP) plywood is made with waterproof adhesives, and is used in damp situations indoors (such as under ceramic floor tiles) as well as for outdoor structures.

Plywood with decorative hardwood outer veneers is used for making furniture and cladding flush doors.

Blockboard A board with a core of softwood strips bonded together edge to edge, and finished with one or two veneer plies on each face.

Blockboard is stronger along the length of the board than across it. It is used mainly for making decorative veneered door blanks, and is hard to find in board form. It is very expensive.

Timberboard A composite board made by gluing together parallel softwood strips to form wide boards suitable for shelving, table tops and worktops as an alternative to blockboard.

The boards are usually 18mm thick, and are intended for staining and varnishing.

Fibreboard and particle board

Hardboard and chipboard were once the most widely used board types, but medium-density fibreboard (known to everyone as MDF) has now taken its place for many DIY projects.

Hardboard Made from heavily-compressed wood fibres, with one smooth surface and one with a mesh texture. It is widely available in just one thickness: 3mm.

Hardboard has little strength, and is mainly used to form the back panels of cabinets and bookcases and the bases of drawers (especially in its white plastic-faced form). It is also used for jobs such as boxing in pipes or lining timber floors where the strength of the board is unimportant. It is possible to get perforated hardboard, which is useful in workshops where tools are to be kept on the wall. Hooks fitted into the holes at the appropriate spots can make a place for every tool.

Also available is oil-tempered hardboard, which is stronger and denser and can be used outdoors.

Chipboard Also known as particle board. Chipboard consists of wood chips bonded together with resins. It has relatively smooth surfaces but rough, crumbly edges that are difficult to finish neatly.

Chipboard is commonly available in 12 and 18mm thicknesses. It is a heavy and dense board that blunts tools quickly, because of its high resin content. It is not as strong as plywood and has poor load-bearing strength – chipboard shelves always tend to sag unless they are well supported – and is mainly used in its plastic-faced form for kitchen units and flat-pack furniture, and in plain 22mm thick sheets for flooring.

Extra-thick 28 and 38mm chipboard forms the core of laminated kitchen worktops.

Medium-density fibreboard (MDF) Made from fine wood fibres bonded together with resin under high pressure to create a board with a fine, even texture and smooth faces and edges. MDF is easier to cut and shape than other board types, and is now widely used for all indoor panel work as well as a wide range of flat-pack furniture.

MDF is available in thicknesses of 6, 9, 12 and 18mm. Cutting, drilling and sanding the board produces a fine dust that can be unpleasant to inhale, so it is advisable to wear a face mask when working with it.

Measuring and marking wood

The first step in making anything using wood or a man-made board is to measure and mark your workpiece so that you can cut it to size. Do this carefully; making a mistake at the start can spoil the entire job.

Starting square

You can generally assume that man-made boards have edges that are square to each other. The same applies to the ends of sawn and planed softwood. However, wood or board offcuts in your workshop may not have square ends or edges, and it is very important to square them up before using them.

1 To check whether an end or edge is square, hold the stock of your try square against the adjacent edge and align the blade with the edge you are checking.

2 If it is not square, move the try square away from the corner by about 5mm and mark a line across the workpiece against the try-square blade with a trimming knife or a sharp pencil.

3 On softwood, use the try square and marker to continue the squared line onto the other faces of the workpiece. The line on the fourth face should meet up with the one on the first face.

4 Cut off the waste to leave a perfectly square end or edge (see page 22).

Measuring

Use a steel ruler for measurements of less than about 300mm, and a tape measure for longer measurements. Always work in millimetres, even if you prefer to think in imperial sizes; it is only too easy to get confused with fractions of an inch, but an exact measurement in millimetres is extremely accurate.

1 Align the end of the ruler with the squared-up end of the workpiece, or hook the end of the tape over the end and extend it as required. Make sure that your eye is vertically above the figure on the ruler or tape that you want to use, and mark the workpiece at that point with a knife or pencil.

2 Hold the try square with its blade aligned with the mark, and square the cutting line across the face of the workpiece. On softwood, continue the line round the workpiece as in step 3, left.

Multiple components

Every saw cut you make removes a small amount of wood, equal to the width of the saw teeth. If you want four pieces of wood each 300mm long and you mark up four successive cutting lines 300mm apart on a length of softwood, each piece will be marginally shorter than 300mm when you cut it off. To avoid this, always mark and cut each component before marking and cutting the next.

You must also allow for the width of the saw cut when marking out man-made boards, ready for cutting into a number of smaller panels. Mark parallel guide lines 3mm apart at the edge of each panel, instead of a single line, so you can saw between the lines when you cut the panels.

Using a combination square

You can use a combination square in the same way as a try square to mark lines at 90° to the edge of the workpiece. It also allows you to mark cutting lines at 45°.

1 Mark the edge of the workpiece where you want the cutting line to begin.

2 Slide the stock to the end of the blade and hold the 45° face against the edge of the workpiece in line with the mark and with the blade extending across its width.

3 Mark the cutting line across the workpiece with a knife or sharp pencil. Alternatively, use the removable scribing pin fitted into the tool's stock.

Using a sliding bevel

A sliding bevel allows you to copy an existing cutting angle – on a replacement staircase baluster, for example – or to set a new angle using a protractor.

1 To copy an existing angle, loosen the wing nut on the tool. Hold the stock against one surface forming the angle and move the blade to touch the other surface. Tighten the wing nut to lock the blade in place.

2 To set a new angle, use a protractor to position the blade at the required angle and lock it in place.

3 Transfer the tool to the workpiece and use it like a try square to transfer the angle of the cutting line to the new wood.

Marking a smooth curve

To mark a perfect circle on any manufactured board, use a batten, a pencil and a nail. Bore a hole at one end of the batten and push in the pencil. Then measure the exact radius of the circle along the batten from the centre of the hole, and drive a nail through it at that point. Pivot the battten on the nail and draw the required circle.

HELPFUL TIP

Select the pencil with care when you're marking measurements on wood. One with a hard lead (marked 1H or higher) will score the wood surface surprisingly deeply, leaving a mark that has to be sanded or even planed off. Use an HB pencil instead. You'll have to sharpen it more often, but the marks it leaves can be removed easily with a soft rubber. A proper carpenter's pencil is the best buy; its flat sides mean it won't roll off the bench. Sharpen it regularly with your trimming knife.

Cutting wood and boards

You can use a hand or power saw to cut wood to length and board panels to size. Power saws save time and effort, but for smaller jobs you may not want the trouble of setting up a power saw. Whichever you use, it is important that the workpiece is held securely so that the saw blade cannot snatch it loose and damage it.

Using a bench hook

The best way of holding mouldings and other small workpieces – up to about 50 x 25mm in size – is to use a bench hook. You can buy one or make one from a piece of timber and two offcuts.

1 Place the lower batten against the near edge of your workbench and place the workpiece against the upper batten. If the batten is inset from the edge of the base, position the cutting line just beyond the end of the batten. If it is not, let the workpiece project beyond the edge of the base by about 25mm.

2 Position the saw blade just on the waste side of the cutting line, guiding it against the side of the thumb of your spare hand. Start the cut with a few light backward strokes of the saw.

3 Saw with the blade at 45° to begin with, then lower it to the horizontal once the cut is established. If the bench hook batten is inset, complete the cut by sawing into the base of the bench hook. This

ensures a clean cut with no splinters on the underside of the workpiece.

If the batten is not inset, complete the cut with gentle strokes to minimise splitting on the underside.

Using a mitre box

You can hold and cut small workpieces in a mitre box, which is itself clamped in the jaws of your workbench. The guide slots in the box allow you to make cuts at 45° as well as at 90°.

1 Mark the cutting line on the workpiece (see pages 20–21). Place it in the box with the cutting line aligned with the slots you want to use. If these do not extend to the base of the box, place a piece of scrap wood beneath the workpiece so that you can saw into it, to avoid a ragged finish.

2 Fit the tenon saw into the slots in the mitre box and use your free hand to hold the workpiece in place. Make the cut with the saw held horizontally. Take care not to widen the slots by letting the saw wander off line.

Using a vice

If you have a woodworking vice, you can use it to hold small workpieces while you cut them. Stick slim packing pieces of scrap wood to the vice jaws with epoxy adhesive to protect the workpiece from being marked by the steel jaws. Never tighten the jaws more than necessary to hold the piece firmly. Soft wood is easily dented.

Using a panel saw

A panel saw is used to cut wood that is too thick for the tenon saw, and to cut man-made boards into smaller panels. It can be used for both cross-cutting (cutting across the grain) and ripping (cutting with the grain). Wood should not be allowed to vibrate while it is being cut, so securing it firmly is essential for a good, clean cut and a satisfactory result.

Even when you take the greatest amount of care, it is possible that the exit cut may be a little rough. To avoid this, always start with the good side of the wood facing upwards in the bench – this way, any minor defects in the cut won't affect the finished job quite as much.

1 To cut wood across the grain, clamp it in the jaws of your workbench with the cutting line clear of the bench frame. Start the cut with a few gentle backwards strokes of the saw blade, then continue cutting with the blade at an angle of about 45°. Hold the offcut with your free hand as you complete the cut to prevent the wood from splintering on the underside.

2 To cut smaller panels from a larger sheet of board, you need to support it on both sides of the cut unless you are sawing close to the board edge. You can rest the panel over the open jaws of your portable workbench and saw between them, but you need to take care not to hit the bench framework. Alternatively, rest the board on two planks supported at each end, or use an open stepladder laid on its side as a makeshift support.

3 Kneel over the workpiece so that your eye is above the cutting line and your arm in line with it. Start the cut on the waste side of the marked line and saw as far as is comfortable. Reposition yourself and the board to continue the cut, and complete it using short saw strokes to avoid splintering the board.

Using a tenon saw

A tenon saw will cut wood and man-made boards. Its cutting depth is limited to about 75mm by the presence of the stiffening along the top edge of the blade. This also limits the width of the workpiece that can be cut; in practice, it is difficult to make a cut longer than about 300mm with this tool.

Whatever you are cutting must be held securely. You can clamp it in the jaws of your workbench. However, it is easier to hold small workpieces using a simple aid called a bench hook (page 14). You can buy one, or make one from scrap wood and board. To make one, glue and screw two pieces of softwood batten to opposite faces of a rectangle of plywood measuring about 250 x 150mm.

1 To cut a piece of wood to length, mark the cutting line on it (see pages 20–21). Hold it securely on your workbench with the thumb of your free hand next to the cutting line to guide the saw blade. Position the saw blade so it will cut just on the waste side of the cutting line, and draw it towards you at about 45° to start the cut.

2 Once the saw teeth begin to bite, start to cut the wood with light but firm strokes. Remember that it cuts on the forward stroke only. Start to flatten out the angle of the saw. Complete the cut with gentle strokes, holding the saw almost level with the wood surface, to avoid splitting the underside of the wood. Support the off-cut with your free hand if the workpiece is held in the jaws of the workbench.

Using a coping saw

If the saw is already fitted with a blade, check the blade tension by tightening the screw-up handle on the tool. To fit a new blade, unscrew the handle fully and unhook the ends of the old blade from their holders. Hook the ends of the new blade into the holders, with the teeth facing away from the handle, and tighten it fully.

1 To make a cut starting at the edge of the workpiece, check that the pins on the blade holders are aligned with the frame. Start the cut with the blade at right angles to the edge. Follow the marked cutting line.

2 As you saw along the cutting line, you may need to rotate the blade to stop the frame from fouling the edge of the workpiece. Unscrew the handle slightly, rotate both blade holder pins to the required angle and re-tighten the handle. Repeat if necessary.

3 To make an internal cut-out, mark its outline and drill a hole through the workpiece within the waste area large enough to admit the saw blade. Unhook the blade from the frame, thread it through the hole and re-attach it to the frame.

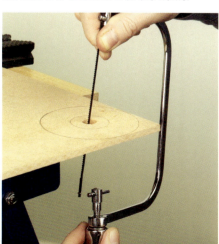

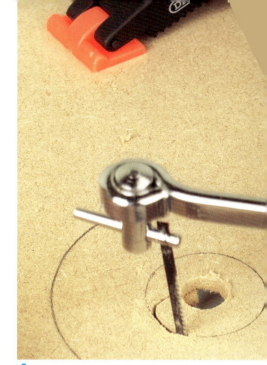

4 Cut from the hole towards the marked outline, then follow it round until you return to your starting point. To allow the blade to turn corners in straight-sided cut-outs, drill a hole within the outline at each corner. Square up the corners with abrasive paper when you have removed the cut-out.

Using a padsaw

The padsaw is ideal for making cut-outs and cutting curves where it is not possible or practicable to use a coping saw. Two typical jobs for it are making cut-outs in plasterboard walls to fit electrical wiring accessories, and cutting keyholes in doors.

Cutting a hole in a wall

1 To make an enclosed cut, mark its outline and drill a starter hole within the waste area big enough to admit the saw blade. If the cut-out is to be square or rectangular, drill a hole at each corner so that you can turn the blade to cut along the next side.

2 Insert the saw blade and start cutting along the marked line. Use short saw strokes in a plasterboard wall to avoid damaging the cladding on the opposite side of the frame.

Cutting a keyhole

To cut a keyhole, drill the starter hole at the top and mark the sides of the slot needed to admit the tongue of the key. Insert the saw blade right through the hole and cut down both sides of the slot. Use a narrow chisel (page 32) to chop out the waste wood, working from both sides of the door.

Using a hole saw

The hole saw will cut perfectly round holes in wood, man-made boards, plasterboard and sheet metal or plastic. Select the blade diameter that matches the hole you want to make and clip it into the circular arbor, or blade holder. Fit the arbor into the chuck of your power drill.

1 Locate the pilot drill bit at the centre of the cut-out and start the drill slowly. As the drill penetrates the surface, the saw teeth will start to cut into it. The cut will be even all round if you are holding the drill at a 90° angle to the surface.

2 If you are cutting a workpiece on your bench, clamp some scrap wood beneath it and saw through the workpiece into the scrap to ensure a clean exit hole.

Using a circular saw

Before you use a circular saw for the first time, read the instructions supplied with it and familiarise yourself with all the controls and safety features. Check that you have the right type of blade for the material you want to cut (see panel on page 26).

1 To remove or change a blade, make sure that the saw is unplugged. Use the Allen key provided with the saw to loosen the retaining nut. For blades with large teeth, jam a screwdriver blade between the saw teeth and the soleplate to stop it turning. For fine blades, hold the saw blade down firmly on some scrap wood. Release the old blade from its spindle, fit the replacement with the teeth pointing forwards and tighten the nut fully.

2 To set the cutting depth you require, place the saw on its side and loosen the lever that locks the saw body to the soleplate. Move the saw body until the saw teeth just project beyond the thickness of the material you are cutting. Tighten the lever again.

3 To make a cut up to about 150mm from the edge of the workpiece, fit the adjustable side fence in its clamp. Set it the required distance from the saw blade and tighten the wing nut. Clamp the workpiece to your workbench.

4 Rest the front edge of the soleplate on the edge of the workpiece and align the narrow guide notch with the marked cutting line. Hold the fence against the side edge of the workpiece.

5 Start the saw and let it run up to full speed, then move it forward until the blade begins to cut. Move the saw forward slowly, with its soleplate flat on the workpiece and the fence running against its side edge.

6 Let the saw run out at the end of the cut before releasing the trigger. Make sure that the blade has stopped before setting the saw down.

7 To make a cut beyond the reach of the fence, clamp a guide batten across the workpiece, parallel with the marked cutting line, and run the edge of the soleplate against it. Align the guide notch with the cutting line and check the position of the batten before starting the cut. Check that the clamps will not foul the saw body as you make the cut.

8 To make an angled cut, loosen the wing nuts at the front and back of the soleplate and rotate the saw body to the setting you want. Lock the nuts and test the cutting angle on some scrap wood.

9 Align the left-hand edge of the wider guide notch on the front of the soleplate with the marked cutting line. Start the saw and feed the blade into the workpiece, then move the saw forward to make the cut. Keep the notch aligned with the cutting line. Remember that cutting depths are reduced when making angled cuts.

CIRCULAR SAW BLADES

Use blades of the correct diameter for your saw. The number of teeth is a general guide to its cutting performance: many small teeth ensure a fine cut; fewer large teeth give a fast but coarse cut. Special blades are available for cutting man-made boards and laminates.

Using a jigsaw

A jigsaw with a 400-500 watt motor is adequate for most DIY tasks, though you may want extra power when you discover how useful this tool is.

A jigsaw will cut wood, man-made boards and several other materials if it is fitted with the correct type of blade. You can buy a basic model very cheaply. Key features to look out for are variable speed, an adjustable soleplate so you can make cuts at angles other than 90°, and some means of collecting or extracting sawdust – either a dust bag or an adaptor so you can

CHOOSING JIGSAW BLADES

Blades for cutting wood and man-made boards come in fine, medium and coarse versions; the closer the teeth, the finer the cut. The maximum cutting depth is usually between 50 and 75mm, depending on the blade. Wood-cutting blades will also cut plastic sheet materials. You need extra-fine blades for cutting metal, and there are also special blades available for cutting ceramic tiles and glass-reinforced plastics (GRP). Check that any blades you buy are compatible with your make of saw; not all are interchangeable between brands.

connect it to a vacuum cleaner. Some jigsaws now feature blade clamps that do not need tools. If the saw is not sold with a carry and storage case, you can buy one from DIY stores to keep the tool safe when you are not using it.

Making a short cut
Select the right blade for the job and fit it in the blade clamp. Secure whatever you are sawing to the workbench with a clamp, or by holding it in the bench jaws. The saw will tend to snatch at the workpiece if you simply hold it with your free hand.

1 You can make short cuts freehand – for example, to cut a wall batten or a piece of skirting board to length. Mark the cutting line and rest the front of the saw's soleplate on the edge of the workpiece.

2 Start the saw at a slow speed and move it forwards so that the blade starts to cut just on the waste side of the cutting line. Make sure the soleplate is flat on the surface of the workpiece.

3 As the cut proceeds, increase the saw speed and check that you are keeping the blade on line. As you complete the cut, support the off-cut with your free hand. Stop the saw as soon as the blade is free.

Making a long straight cut
Because the saw blade is narrow, it can wander off-line on long, straight cuts made freehand. On thick materials, there is also a tendency for the blade to deform under load, giving a cut that is not at 90° to the surface of the workpiece. To prevent the first problem, use a saw guide. To counteract the second, let the saw cut at its own speed rather than forcing it.

1 If the jigsaw is supplied with a side fence – a tee-shaped bar projecting from the side of the soleplate – you can use it to make cuts up to about 150mm from the edge of the workpiece. Clamp the fence in the required position and make a test cut on some scrap wood to check the setting.

2 Position the saw so the blade is aligned with the cutting line and the fence lies against the edge of the wood.

3 Move the saw forwards as the cut proceeds, keeping the fence against the edge of the workpiece. Allow the blade to run out of the cut at the far end.

Using a guide batten
To make a cut further from the edge of the workpiece than the fence will allow, use a guide batten. This is a strip of wood clamped across the workpiece to guide the edge of the saw's soleplate along the cut.

1 Mark the cutting line, align the saw blade with it and place the batten next to the side of the soleplate.

2 When you are happy with its position, clamp it to the workpiece and check that the clamps will not interfere with the travel of the saw. Make the cut by running the edge of the soleplate against the batten.

Making a curved cut

Mark the cutting line on the workpiece. Avoid starting a curved cut at the edge; the blade will skate off it as you try to start the cut. Instead, drill a hole in the waste area large enough to admit the saw blade and begin the cut there.

1 Start the cut as for a straight cut, positioning the blade on the waste side of the cutting line. Move the saw forward at its own speed – don't attempt to push it – following the cutting line by eye.

2 Cut more slowly on sharp curves, turning the saw body gradually so the blade can follow it closely. In this instance, the curve was a continuation of a straight cut, so no starter hole was required.

Making an internal cut-out

Mark the cut-out on the workpiece; if you are cutting a square or a rectangle, draw a line in from each corner at 45°. You will be placing the point of the drill bit on this line.

1 If you use a 16mm spade bit, place the point of the bit at least 8mm into the waste area from the corner, on the 45° line. Drill all four holes.

2 Insert the saw blade and rest the soleplate on the workpiece. Follow the cutting line to the next drill hole for straight cuts, or carry on cutting round a curve.

3 At the next corner, let the saw blade run right into the angle. Then turn the blade in the drill hole and start the next straight cut. Repeat at the third corner to run the saw back to your starting point.

4 Use abrasive paper to smooth the edges of the cut and to square up the internal corners.

Drilling wood

Almost every woodworking project involves drilling holes, and much of this will be done on your workbench.

You can either use a cordless drill or a corded drill. The corded drill has the advantage of higher drilling speeds which allow you to work faster and more accurately, and the extra power means that you can drill bigger holes than a cordless drill can manage. It will also drill large or deep holes in dense masonry that are beyond the capacity of a cordless drill. It is, however, essential to clamp your workpiece to the bench before carrying out any drilling operation because power of the drill can snatch a hand-held workpiece from your grasp. For more information on cordless drills, see page 11.

Get to know your drill

Mains drills have power ratings in watts (W), ranging from about 500W for small single-speed drills up to 750W or more for big semi-professional models. Most have variable speed control from 0 to about 3000rpm; some have two speed ranges. The more powerful drills have the advantage of a 13mm chuck (most cordless drills have only a 10mm chuck) that will take larger-diameter twist and masonry drill bits.

Before you use the drill for the first time, read the instructions. These will tell you how to select the following:
• The correct speed setting for the material you are drilling, screwdriving and, if the drill has the option, hammer action for making holes in masonry.
• Drilling, hammer-drilling or screwdriving.
• The correct torque setting (if available) which enables you to apply the optimum turning force when driving screws into different materials.
• Forward or reverse gear (for removing screws and freeing jammed drill bits).

Most drills come with a carry case; keep the drill in it when you are not using it. If you do not have a case, buy one. DIY stores stock a selection, so take your drill in to test its fit before you buy.

CHECK THE BATTERIES

Cordless drills run on rechargeable batteries, and all but the cheapest come with two batteries. Make sure you know how to remove and insert the batteries, and how to operate the battery charger. Check whether the battery can be left to trickle-charge for hours, or whether it has a fixed recharge time.

Fitting drill bits

Select the right type of drill bit for the job you are doing (pages 10–11).

1 Open the chuck by twisting the knurled ring and fit the end of the drill bit inside it.

2 Tighten the locking ring until you feel it start to slip. The drill bit is now secure. Select forward gear and the drilling or hammer-drilling option, and you are ready to start work.

Drilling freehand

To drill holes simply point the drill at the surface and squeeze the trigger. Most drilled holes must be at 90° to the surface.

1 If you have a good eye, check from two angles that you are holding the drill at more or less the right angle. This is good enough for many drilling jobs.

2 If you want to check the angle more accurately, hold the drill in position and set a try square against the surface you are drilling into. The drill bit should be parallel with the metal blade of the try square.

DRILL BITS YOU MAY NOT HAVE ALREADY

Dowel drill bits These resemble twist drill bits, but have a centre point and cutting spurs (like a miniature flat wood bit) that enable them to drill holes more accurately than a twist drill bit when making dowel joints (page 44). They are available in 6, 8 and 10mm diameters to match ready-cut hardwood dowel sizes.

Auger drill bits Used to drill deep holes in wood up to 25mm in diameter, for which a flat wood bit would be too inaccurate. They have a screw-threaded lead point and a cutting spur, with deep spiral flutes to clear the debris from the hole. They are available in diameters up to 25mm, in two lengths – 100 and 200mm.

End mill bits Used to drill shallow stopped holes such as those required when fitting recessed cabinet hinges and certain assembly fittings (pages 67–71). They come in a range of sizes, but the most widely used sizes are 25, 26 and 35mm.

Drilling small holes in wood

Fit a twist drill bit of the required diameter and select the drilling setting on the drill.

1 Secure the workpiece on your workbench, with some scrap wood underneath if you are drilling a hole right through it. This prevents you from damaging your bench jaws, and also guarantees a clean exit hole through the workpiece.

2 Hold the drill tip at the mark and check that you are holding it upright. Drill the hole through the workpiece and on into the scrap wood.

Drilling large holes in wood

Fit a flat wood bit of the required size and select the drilling setting on the drill.

1 Secure the workpiece on the bench with scrap wood beneath it.

2 Position the lead point of the drill bit at the mark and start drilling. As the cutting blades begin to bite and cut the hole, they will cut evenly if you are holding the drill upright. Drill on into the scrap wood, which will guarantee a clean exit hole through the workpiece.

Alternatively Clamp the wood so the drill can emerge from the underside into free air. Drill the hole until the lead point just penetrates the wood. Turn it over, locate the lead point in the hole and drill out the rest of the hole. This will reduce the risk of leaving a rough exit hole.

Drill bit varieties

Apart from the basic selection of drill bits outlined on page 10, you may need to buy others for specific DIY jobs.

Long twist drills are available in lengths of up to 165mm (and 8mm in diameter). They are used for making holes in thick components such as timber-framed partition walls.

Reduced-shank drills are available in diameters up to 20mm (most standard twist drills go up to 10 or 13mm only). They have 13mm diameter shanks to fit the maximum chuck size on most cordless drills.

Using a drill stand

A drill stand holds the drill in a movable clamp mounted on a vertical pillar. It can be clamped in place on your workbench, or can be bolted to it if you have a permanent bench rather than a portable one. The stand allows you to drill holes at precisely 90° to the surface of the workpiece, which is placed on the stand's base. This accuracy is particularly important for jobs such as making dowel joints or drilling the recesses in cabinet doors for spring-loaded hinges.

The stand can also be set up to allow you to drill stopped holes to a precise depth.

Take your drill with you when you shop for a drill stand, to ensure that it will fit in the clamp. Some drill stands will not accept drills with keyless chucks.

1 Mount the drill in the stand and fit the drill bit you want to use (see page 10 and panel opposite). Check the travel of the drill in the stand to ensure that the drill bit will penetrate the workpiece without drilling into the bench beneath the stand's base.

2 Place the workpiece beneath the drill and lower the drill bit so it just touches the surface. Adjust its position until the bit is at the drilling mark; then clamp the workpiece to the bench.

3 Set the depth of travel on the stand if you want to drill a stopped hole. Test the result on some scrap wood first.

4 Raise the drill, squeeze the trigger and lock it on. Lower it and drill the hole, then raise the drill while it is still running to clear sawdust from the hole. Release the trigger lock.

Shaping wood by hand

Most of the wood you use will be in standard sizes or will be a ready-machined moulding, and the range of sizes and cross-sections available will meet most of your requirements.

Sometimes, however, you need to shape a piece of wood for a particular purpose. Chisels, rasps and Surforms will help you to do this. If you need a component that is not available as a standard size or profile, you will have to alter its cross-section or shape. For this you need a plane and a router respectively. You can cut curves with a suitable saw (see pages 24 and 28). Rounded ends or surfaces curved in more than one direction need another approach.

Paring with a chisel

The simplest way to form a rounded end or corner is to trim (pare) it with a chisel.

1 Mark the shape you want to cut on your workpiece. Clamp it securely on your workbench, with some scrap wood or board underneath it to protect the bench surface. Cut off the bulk of the area with a saw before you use the chisel.

2 Use a sharpened chisel (see page 15) to pare the remaining wood. Continue trimming off finer and finer shavings until you have cut back to the marked line.

3 Smooth the resulting curve with a fine rasp (see below) and then abrasive paper.

Shaping with a wood rasp

A rasp is often confused with a file, which is a metalworking tool and has parallel cutting edges machined across its blade. Rasp blades have individual raised teeth, which remove wood in the same manner as a very coarse abrasive paper. The tool cuts on the forward stroke. If the teeth become clogged with wood fibres as you work, clean them with a wire brush.

1 Mark the curve you want to shape on the workpiece, and clamp it securely in a vice or the jaws of your workbench.

2 Hold the handle in one hand and place the tool on the wood. Steady the tip of the blade with your other hand to keep the blade flat on the surface.

3 Push the tool forwards to start shaping the wood, repeating the stroke and moving the contact point round the curve as you work to create the required shape.

4 To shape a concave curve, use a round rasp or the rounded face of a half-round rasp and work from both sides of the workpiece to prevent splintering.

Shaping with a Surform

A Surform is a rasp with a difference, having individual cutting teeth stamped out of a thin steel sheet. Different tools in the range have a blade that is flat, gently rounded, curved along its length or rolled into a cylinder, and each is used in a different way. The blades are replaceable.

1 Hold the tool parallel with the wood grain and push it along the wood in a series of steady strokes.

2 Clear shavings from the inside of the blade from time to time. As you near the shape you want, turn the tool slightly to alter the cutting angle and produce finer shavings.

HELPFUL TIP

There are different Surforms for specific jobs. Use a half-round blade to shape concave curves, as for a rasp (see step 4 left). Use a round file to shape tight curves and holes – again work from both sides of the wood to avoid splintering. The Surform shaver tool has a smaller blade, and is designed to cut on the pull stroke. Use it in tight corners where the larger tools cannot reach.

Using a plane

A bench (jack) plane about 350mm long is used to reduce the cross-section of wood from an off-the-peg size to the dimensions required. Its blade must be sharp to cut the wood cleanly (see page 15) and must be correctly adjusted.

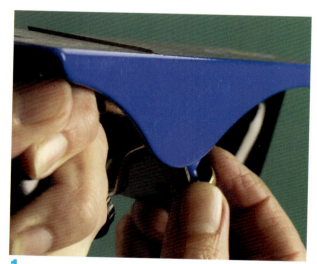

1 Sight along the soleplate of the plane to check that the blade is set square to it, and that it projects by the correct distance. Use the lateral adjustment lever behind the blade to set the cutting edge squarely, and the knurled nut between blade and handle to alter the blade projection.

2 Mark the cutting line on both faces of the workpiece and clamp it securely in your workbench. Hold the plane on the near end of the workpiece and use your free hand to grasp the front handle. Press the fingers of this hand against the side of the workpiece to guide the plane along its edge.

3 Plane from one end of the workpiece to the other in smooth, steady strokes. Let the plane run off the wood at each end of the stroke. Regularly check your progress towards the marked lines. Remove shavings from the jaws as you work.

Using a power planer

A power planer is useful for re-sizing work as well as jobs such as fitting new doors. Read the instructions and ensure you know how to fit and change the cutting blades.

For general bench work, use the planer in the same way as a bench plane. If you are working on a door, fit the guide fence to the planer and clamp the door on your portable workbench so you can plane the ends and edges as shown below.

1 Mark cutting lines on the workpiece, set the cutting depth on the planer and fit the fence.

HELPFUL TIP

If you buy a power planer, look out for these useful features:
A V-groove running down the centre of the sole plate allows you to chamfer (take the sharp edge off) the edge of doors and other fixtures.
A flip-down guard prevents the blades from being damaged by contact with any surface on which the planer is laid.

2 Place the front of the soleplate against the end of the door with the fence resting on its face, and switch the tool on. Move it forwards, guiding it with both hands.

3 As you complete each pass, let the planer run off the end of the workpiece. Repeat until you reach the marked lines.

4 You can use a power planer to chamfer edges at 45° too, by letting the groove in the soleplate run along the edge of the workpiece. Mark guide lines on each face of the work and plane down to them.

Using a router

Depending on which accessories and bits you fit, you can use a router to create edge profiles, grooves and recesses in solid wood and in man-made boards – MDF takes routed effects especially well. The bit rotates at extremely high speed, so the tool needs careful handling. Read the instructions and practise on some scrap before tackling your first job.

Setting up the router

1 To fit your selected cutting bit, use the spanner and locking pin provided. Place the router on its side and lock the chuck (called the collet) with the pin. Loosen the collet with the spanner and insert the bit as far as it will go. Tighten the collet fully and remove the locking pin.

2 To set the routing depth, stand the router on the workbench and undo the winged nut securing the depth rod so it is free to move. Loosen the side handle, press the body of the router down until the bit touches the bench surface and tighten the handle again.

3 Read off the value indicated on the depth scale and add the required routing depth to it. Set the pointer on the depth rod to this combined figure and tighten the winged nut below the scale. Loosen the side handle and allow the router body to rise up on its springs. Check that the routing depth is correct by making a test cut on some scrap wood.

4 If the machine has a dust extractor facility, fit the adaptor and connect it to the hose of your vacuum cleaner.

Routing an edge profile

The router cutter rotates counter-clockwise when viewed from above the tool. Always feed the cutter into the wood from the right, so it is turning into the wood it is about to cut away. If you work in the opposite direction, the speed of the machine may wrench it from your grasp with some force, and you are likely to damage your work.

1 Select the cutter you want to use and fit it in the collet. Set the cutting depth required (see step 2, below left). Clamp the work securely to your workbench, and check that the clamps will not impede the router as you move it along the edge.

2 Rest the edge of the soleplate on top of the workpiece. Switch the router on, press the body down on its springs and guide it sideways into the edge you are shaping. Cut in until the guide pin touches the edge of the workpiece.

3 Move the router slowly forwards, with the baseplate flat on the surface of the workpiece. Let the cutter run off at the far end of the cut and switch off the power.

Using a guide fence

To machine a groove parallel with the edge of the workpiece, fit the guide fence to the router soleplate using the guide plates and winged screws. Mark the position of the groove on the workpiece and set the cutting depth required.

1 Place the router on the workpiece with the cutter aligned with the marked line. Move the fence in against the edge of the workpiece and tighten the securing screws.

2 Position the router soleplate on the end of the workpiece with the fence pressed against its edge. Start the motor, loosen the side handle and press the router body down to the pre-set cutting depth. Tighten the handle again.

3 Start the motor and move the router forwards slowly to cut the groove. Keep the fence pressed against the edge of the workpiece. Let the cutter run out at the end of the groove and switch off the motor.

Using a guide batten

If you want to cut grooves further in from the edge of the workpiece than the fence will allow, use a guide batten instead (see page 27). Clamp it across the workpiece and guide the flat side of the router soleplate against it as you machine the groove. Check that the clamps will not impede the movement of the router.

Choosing router bits

Bits for DIY routers usually have 6mm diameter shafts and tungsten carbide cutting tips. Grooving cutters are plain, while shaping (edge) cutters have a guide wheel that runs against the edge of the workpiece and stops the bit from cutting too deeply. You can buy bits singly, but it is better to buy a set complete with a storage case.

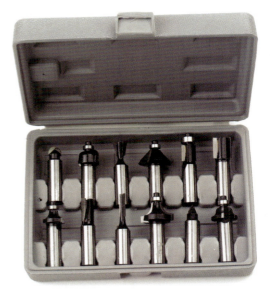

Nailing

A nail is one of the simplest fixing devices. Its point is driven through whatever you are fixing and on into the material beneath until its head is flush with the surface. Different nail types and sizes are used for different jobs, but you will need only a small range to cope with everyday DIY jobs – see Choosing nails, page 38. Use a claw or pin hammer to drive nails in.

Using a claw hammer

A claw hammer will drive all but the smallest nails with ease, and its claw will extract nails that are misaligned or bent while being driven in. Hold it near the end of the handle and watch the hammer head to make sure that it strikes the nail head squarely.

1 Hold the nail between your thumb and forefinger and start it with a few gentle taps of the hammer head. Check that it is at right angles to the surface.

2 Release the nail and drive it in with harder blows. For large nails, keep your wrist stiff and swing hammer and forearm from the elbow. On rough work, hammer the nail head in flush with the surface.

Using a pin hammer

A pin hammer or lightweight ball-pein hammer (shown here) is easier to handle when driving small panel pins, tacks, upholstery nails and glazing sprigs (used to hold glass panes in wooden window frames).

1 Hold the pin between your thumb and forefinger and tap it in with the flat end of the hammer head.

2 When it stands by itself, drive it in with the hammer head, flexing your wrist to control the hammer. Drive the pin fully home, or use a nail punch to recess its head in the wood, if necessary.

Choosing nails

The two nail types you are likely to use most frequently are oval wire nails and panel pins. For everyday fixings, keep a supply of these in a compartmentalised storage box. Buy other types of nail as and when you need them.

Oval wire nails Have an oval cross-section and a stubby head. These are the most commonly used nails. Position them with the oval parallel with the wood grain to avoid splitting the wood. Punch in the nail head and fill over it for an invisible fixing. Use these nails for securing the joints in light timber frames, and for other general woodwork jobs.
Sizes From 25 to 150mm; useful sizes to keep are 50 and 75mm.

Panel pins Have a round cross-section and a small flat head. As the name implies, they are used chiefly for fixing thin sheet materials to an underlying timber framework. They are also ideal for fixing timber mouldings in place, although pilot holes for the pins may be needed in small mouldings to avoid splitting the wood. Hardboard panel pins have a diamond-shaped head that is driven in flush with the board surface, and often have a coppered finish.
Sizes From 15 to 50mm; useful sizes to keep are 20, 25 and 40mm.

Round wire nails Have a round cross-section and a large flat head. They are used on rough woodwork, such as the framework for a partition wall or a garden pergola.
Sizes From 25 to 150mm.

Cut nails Traditional nails cut from flat metal sheet. Cut clasp nails are still used to fix wood to masonry (skirting boards, for example), while cut floor nails – also known as floor brads – are used to fix floorboards to their joists.
Sizes Various sizes are available.

Annular (ring-shank) nails Have a ridged shank which grips wood better than a smooth wire nail. They are used in situations where the fixing has to resist being pulled apart, and are almost impossible to remove once driven. They are particularly good for making fixings into man-made boards.
Sizes From 20 to 100mm.

Plasterboard nails Have a cone-shaped head (like a countersunk screw) and a jagged shank to grip the framing to which the board is being fixed. They have a galvanised finish.
Sizes 30 and 40mm, for fixing 9.5 and 12.7mm thick plasterboard respectively.

Fixing with screws

A screw is a stronger fixing device than a nail. Its thread grips the material into which it is driven, and its head secures the item being fixed. Unlike a nail, a screw can be withdrawn easily to undo the fixing.

As with nails, different types and sizes of screws are used for different jobs. You will need a screwdriver to drive screws, and to work successfully the screwdriver tip must match the size and shape of the recess in the screw head. You can drive (and remove) screws by hand, or with a cordless screwdriver or drill.

Screwing wood to wood

Start by choosing a screw with a countersunk head that is long enough to pass through the piece you are fixing, and halfway through the piece you are fixing it to. The screw head will be flush with the surface once the screw has been driven in. Screws come in different diameters called gauge numbers, but for most jobs you will need only two. Gauge 8 screws up to 50mm long will be thick enough for most jobs; use a thicker gauge 10 screw up to 75mm long for heavier-duty fixings.

1 Mark where you want the screw hole in the piece of wood. Fit a twist drill bit the same size as the screw shank in your drill, and drill a hole through the wood. Place scrap wood beneath the workpiece so you do not drill into your workbench.

2 Exchange the twist drill bit for a countersink bit and drill the cone-shaped recess for the screw head in the mouth of the clearance hole. It should be as wide as the screw head.

3 Hold the piece of wood you are fixing in position over the piece you are fixing it to. Push a nail (or a bradawl if you have one) through the clearance hole you drilled in step 1 to mark the screw position on the piece below. Drill a pilot hole 2mm in diameter at the mark, to half the depth of the wood.

4 Reposition the two pieces of wood and insert the screw through the clearance hole in the top piece so it enters the pilot hole in the piece beneath. Tighten it fully with your screwdriver until the screw head is fully recessed in the countersunk hole.

Screwing metal to wood

Most metal fixtures – such as door handles, window catches, coat hooks and shelf supports – have countersunk holes for their fixing screws.

You can use a countersunk screw to attach them, but screws with raised countersunk heads look more attractive. They are available in brass, chrome and stainless steel, and matching screws are often supplied with the fixture.

If you have to supply your own, make sure the screw shank will pass through the clearance holes in the fixture. The screws should be long enough to pass halfway through the wood you are fixing into.

Door hinges are an exception; they are always fixed with countersunk screws.

Some metal fixtures – particularly those used out of doors, such as gate hinges – do not have countersinks, and are fixed with round-head screws. The hemispherical screw heads sit proud of the surface.

1 Decide where you are going to position the fixture. Hold the fixture in position and mark each screw position on the wood in pencil through the clearance holes.

2 Drill a 2mm pilot hole at each mark, to half the thickness of the wood. If you find it difficult to gauge the depth, use a strip of masking tape as a guide on the drill bit. Stop when the guide touches the wood.

3 Replace the fixture over the holes and drive in the screws. If there is more than one, only tighten them fully when you are sure the fixture is straight and level.

Screwing into walls

You cannot simply drive a screw into most walls to make a fixing. The only exception to this is if you have a timber-framed partition wall and the fixing position coincides with one of the vertical frame members. Otherwise you have to drill a hole and insert a special fixing device to hold the screw in place.

Using a power screwdriver

Driving screws with a power screwdriver is much quicker and easier than driving them by hand, especially when using cross-head screws. You can use a cordless drill on a slow speed setting, or buy a cordless screwdriver instead. Both tools use interchangeable screwdriver bits, which are available to fit all common screw heads. It is actually cheaper to buy a set of these bits and a cordless tool than it is to buy individual screwdrivers. You can use a power driver with slotted-head screws, but there is a greater risk of the bit slipping out of the slot and damaging the workpiece than with hand screwdriving.

1 Select the screwdriver bit to match the screw size and recess type. Fit it in the drill chuck, or use the magnetic bit holder supplied with the bits.

2 If you are using a cordless drill, set it to the screwdriving symbol and choose an intermediate torque setting (for example, 3 on a scale of 1 to 5).

3 Fit the screw into the tip of the screwdriver bit and offer it up to its pre-drilled hole.

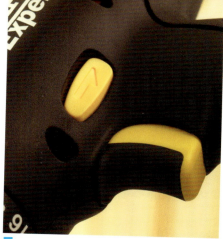

4 Start the drill or screwdriver and drive in the screw. With a cordless drill, the torque setting selected should allow the clutch to slip as the screw is tightened. If this does not happen, select a different torque setting until it does.

5 Set the screwdriver or drill to reverse to undo a screw.

Choosing screws

Most of the fixings you make will require countersunk screws. Traditionally, all screws had slotted heads and were driven with a flat-tip screwdriver. Today, screws are designed for driving with a power screwdriver, and their heads have a specially shaped recess to engage the screwdriver tip more positively than a flat-tip driver does in a slot. The most common recesses are cross-shaped.

Round-head Pozidriv

Round-head slotted

Countersunk slotted

Countersunk Pozidriv

Countersunk Pozidriv

Countersunk Pozidriv

Phillips These screws have a simple cross, and are found mainly in flat-pack furniture kits and on domestic appliances.

Pozidriv and Prodrive A star-shaped recess grips the screwdriver tip more securely than a slotted head. Drivers for Pozidriv and Prodrive screws are interchangeable. In each case the No. 2 size will drive screws up to gauge 10.

Woodscrews Traditional woodscrews are threaded only for part of their length. Many modern countersunk screws have continuously-threaded shanks and other features such as twin threads that are designed to make them quicker and easier to drive.

For everyday use, store a small selection of Pozidriv or Prodrive countersunk woodscrews in individual containers. The most useful sizes are: 19, 25, 38 and 50mm in gauge No. 8; 50 and 75mm in gauge No. 10.

Other screw head types Raised countersunk and round-head woodscrews usually have slotted heads. Other head types you may encounter – especially in flat-pack furniture kits and on domestic appliances – include internal-hex screws with a plain hexagonal recess, driven with an Allen key; Torx screws and Uni-screws with specially shaped hexagonal recesses; Robertson screws with a square recess. Each type requires a special screwdriver.

Making joints

Joining wood to wood is an essential skill to master, but you do not need the skills of a cabinet-maker to make a good job. The type of joint you choose will depend on how strong you want it to be, and on how important its appearance is. This section will help you to make those choices, and demonstrate some basic skills that will be useful for a wide range of woodworking projects.

Basic joints

Butt joints These are the easiest joints to make. They are formed by aligning the two components (such as the sides of a box) so that the edge of one overlaps the end of the other. Butt joints can also be used to join wood edge to edge – to make a table top, for example. There are several options for joining the components:
• Fix the corner joint together with nails or screws and strengthen with wood glue.
• Reinforce a corner or edge joint with hardwood dowels or oval-shaped slips of compressed wood called biscuits.
• Use one of the ingenious assembly fittings that were originally designed for use in flat-pack furniture (page 70).
• Use a metal angle bracket or a corrugated fastener (below), although these remain visible unless you take steps to hide them.

Mitre joints Butt joints that meet at a 45° angle are called mitre joints. They are used mainly in frames where the appearance of the corner joint is important – in a picture frame, for example, or where the architrave mouldings round a door opening meet. Like butt joints they can be nailed, screwed, dowel-jointed or biscuit-jointed, and are usually glued as well.

Halving joints As their name implies, halving joints are made by cutting away half of each component so they fit together neatly. The joint is stronger than a butt joint because the parts interlock. If the joint is also glued, it is even stronger because the glued contact area between the parts is bigger. The joint is usually nailed or screwed. Halving joints are used mainly in frames, and components can be joined in L, T or X shapes. The last two – called tee halving joints and cross halving joints respectively – need a slot cut in one or both components (see pages 46–47).

Mortise-and-tenon joints These are serious woodworking joints, formed by fitting a shaped peg (the tenon) into a matching slot (the mortise). They are used mainly in fine furniture making, and are also found in framed doors, sash windows and the like.

Using a try square to mark up joints

The most important feature of any woodworking joint is that it should be square, and the try square (page 9) is the tool to use for checking this. You also need a try square for marking cutting lines at 90°, both when cutting wood to length and when marking out halving joints.

1 Mark where you want to cut your workpiece to length. Hold the stock of the try square against its edge at the mark, with the blade across the width, and mark the line with a trimming knife or sharp pencil.

2 Turn the workpiece through 90°, align the try square with the marked line on its face and mark the line on its edge. Repeat the process to continue the marked line all the way round the workpiece. This continuous line will help you to cut the wood squarely to length.

3 To mark out a corner halving joint, clamp the two pieces together and check with the try square that they are at 90° to each other. Mark the edge of each piece on the face of the other.

4 Separate the two pieces and use the try square to continue the marked lines onto the edge of each piece.

Using a marking gauge

To mark out a halving joint, you need a marking gauge (page 9). This enables you to mark the thickness of the wood you want to cut away from each component to make the joint.

1 Loosen the thumbscrew on the block and slide it along the beam so the pin is approximately half the thickness of the workpiece away from the block. Tighten the screw.

2 Hold the block against one face of the workpiece and mark the edge with the pin. Then hold it against the opposite face and repeat the mark. If they coincide, the gauge is correctly set. If they do not, move the block slightly and repeat the process until they do. Tighten the screw fully.

3 Hold the block against the face of each component in turn, and slide it along so the pin marks the halving line on each edge of each component, extending to the end from the cutting line you marked with the try square.

4 Join the edge marks across the end grain of each component. Then cross-hatch the area to be cut away in pencil on each component, ready for the joint to be cut.

Using a mortise gauge

The mortise gauge has two pins, one of which is movable, and is designed for marking the width of a mortise on the edge of the workpiece. You set the pin separation first to match the width of the tenon (or the lock body). You then position the block so the two pins mark the mortise in the centre of the edge, in the same way as using a marking gauge to mark a centre line when marking out a halving joint. However, most woodworkers today drill out mortises with a flat wood bit that matches the mortise width, rather than cutting them with a chisel, so there is no need to mark it in the traditional way.

Making dowel joints

The positions of the dowel holes must be carefully matched in the two components being joined. Use a drill bit that matches readily available sizes of hardwood dowel – commonly 6 or 8mm in diameter. It's a good idea to use a drill stand or a dowelling jig to ensure that the holes are drilled at precise right angles to the face of the workpiece, and to the correct depth.

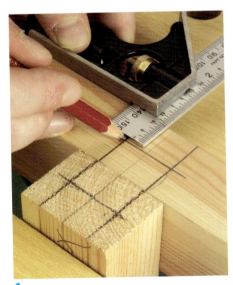

1 Use a combination square to mark a centre line on the end or edge of the first component to be drilled. Mark the dowel positions on this line and corresponding marks on the second component.

2 Drill a hole at each cross in the first component, making the holes a little deeper than half the length of the dowel. Use a drill stand or clamp the dowelling jig to the workpiece and use it to guide the drill bit.

3 Squeeze some wood glue into the holes and insert the dowels. Drill the dowel holes in the second component, ready for the joint to be assembled.

4 Check the alignment of the two components before squeezing some glue into the holes and assembling the joint.

5 Use a wooden mallet to drive the dowels home. Wipe away any surplus adhesive with a damp cloth.

Making biscuit joints

You need a power tool called a biscuit jointer to cut the slots for the biscuits in the two components. Follow the instructions supplied with the tool to cut the slots. Then squirt woodworking adhesive into the slots, insert the biscuits and assemble the joint. Clamp the joint until the adhesive has set.

Making mitre joints

You can cut mitre joints freehand after marking the cutting angles with a combination square (see advice on using a try square on page 9), or by using a protractor and ruler. Alternatively, you can use a mitre box (page 8) to guide the saw. For the best results a mitre saw (page 9) is the ideal tool to use.

1 Mark the joint positions on each component. Set the cutting angle to 45° by rotating the saw's baseplate, then lock it.

2 Clamp the workpiece in place on the base of the mitre saw and lower the saw blade to check that the cut will be aligned with the mark. Then make the cut. Repeat for the other component of the joint.

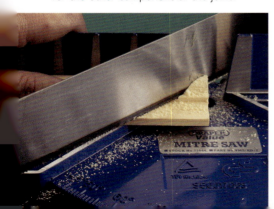

3 Apply adhesive to one mitred end and assemble the joint. Check that it is square, set it aside and leave it until the adhesive has set. You can reinforce the joint by driving a panel pin or a screw in from each side of the joint, or you can drill holes in each mitred face to take dowels. You can also reinforce mitre joints with biscuits (see above). Special cramps are available that will hold the joint accurately while the adhesive sets.

Making corner halving joints

Once you have marked out the two components (page 43), you can cut and assemble the joint. You need a tenon saw and some wood adhesive (or a glue gun).

1 Clamp each component on its edge and, starting the cut at an angle, begin to saw along the grain.

2 Then complete the cut down to the shoulder marks, holding the saw blade at right-angles to the workpiece.

3 Using a bench hook (page 14) to steady the workpiece, cut carefully across the width to form the shoulder.

4 Squirt some adhesive onto the cut faces of one component and assemble the joint. Clamp it for maximum bond strength, with cardboard or scrap wood between the clamp jaws and the workpieces to prevent dents. Use your try square to check that the joint is a perfect right angle. Wipe away excess adhesive with a damp cloth.

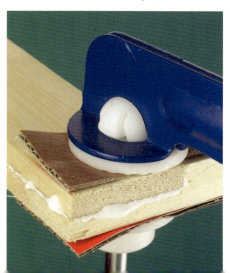

Making tee halving joints

As with a corner halving joint, use the two components you wish to join to mark the outline of the joint.

1 Clamp the two components together, check that they are at right angles and mark the edges of each component on the face of the other one.

2 Use a marking gauge to mark the joint thickness on the edge of each component. Cut the piece forming the leg of the tee in the same way as for a corner halving joint (page 45).

3 Using a tenon saw, make two parallel cuts on the waste side of the marks on the piece forming the cross-bar of the tee. Saw down to the halfway line. Then make several more cuts to the same depth within the waste area.

4 Clamp the workpiece securely and, using a sharp chisel, begin to chisel out the waste wood between the outer saw cuts.

5 Work from opposite sides in turn so as to avoid splintering, until the base of the notch is flat and is level with the halfway lines on the edges.

6 Test the fit of the two components, and shave away any excess wood with your chisel if necessary.

7 Glue and assemble the joint as for a corner halving joint (page 45).

Making cross halving joints

Mark out the joint from the two components as before, then use your tenon saw and chisel to create two matching notches as for cutting the cross-piece of a tee halving joint. Test the fit and assemble the joint as before.

FORMING MORTISES

Mortise joints are mainly used in professional woodworking, such as the production of fine furniture. The only time you are likely to need a mortise is when installing a mortise lock in a front or back door.

Smoothing wood

Whether you are working with wood or man-made boards, you will need to sand the surface smooth before you can apply a decorative finish to it. Do this by hand, or use one of the many different power sanders now available.

Sanding by hand

The traditional way of smoothing wood is to wrap a piece of abrasive paper round a cork sanding block and to rub it along the direction of the grain. Sanding across the grain can leave scratches which are difficult to remove and can mar a clear finish. Glasspaper (often incorrectly still called sandpaper) is the cheapest sheet abrasive available, but aluminium oxide abrasives cut better and last longer. Both types are sold in standard 280 x 230mm sheets.

Glasspaper Made in a series of grades: 3, 2½ and S2 are coarse; M2, F2 and 1½ are medium; 1, 0 and 00 are fine.

Aluminium oxide paper Graded by numbers, running from 40, 50 and 60 (coarse) through 80, 100 and 120 (medium) to 150, 180 and beyond (fine).

You will usually need only fine grades for finishing planed timber and board surfaces, but you may need other grades for smoothing cut ends and board edges.

Note that silicon carbide abrasive paper, also known as wet-and-dry paper, is not intended for use in sanding bare wood. Its main DIY use is for smoothing metal and keying existing painted or varnished surfaces prior to redecoration.

Power sanding

Disc sanding attachments (used with a power drill) can leave tell-tale scratches. Integral power sanders give better results. Different types do different jobs. A random-orbit sander will cope with most everyday sanding jobs. You can buy a basic tool quite cheaply. All use aluminium oxide abrasive sheets, graded as for hand abrasives (see below).

Key features to look for are a 125mm diameter sanding pad, a locking switch for continuous operation, and some form of dust extraction via a dust bag or vacuum cleaner attachment. Most sanders now use touch-and-close (Velcro) fastenings to attach the abrasive discs to the sanding pad. However, these are comparatively expensive.

CHOOSING ABRASIVES

The sanding discs for this type of sander use aluminium oxide grit as the abrasive, bonded to a strong backing fabric. If the sander has a through-the-pad dust extraction system, the sheets have holes in them that coincide with holes in the sanding pad, allowing the machine to draw dust up through the pad as you work. Make sure that the discs you buy are compatible with your make of sander; not all brands are interchangeable.

There is a range of disc grades, from coarse, for fast removal of material, to extra fine for finishing work. Some brands use a numbering system to indicate the coarseness of the abrasive grit; the lower the number, the coarser the grit. Typical figures are 180 (coarse), 240 (medium) and 400 (fine).

Using a random-orbit sander

This sander is the simplest of all power tools to use. Its action is designed to leave no scratch marks on the surface of wood when used with a fine grade abrasive disc.

1 Select the correct grade of abrasive disc for the finish you want to achieve, and attach it to the sanding pad so the holes in disc and pad are aligned. Press the disc firmly into place on the pad.

2 Connect the sander to the hose of your vacuum cleaner using the adaptor provided, and switch the vacuum cleaner on. Alternatively, fit the dust bag if the tool has one.

3 Hold the disc against the surface you want to sand and switch on the power. Keep the sander moving backwards and forwards over the surface.

4 Be prepared to switch discs as you work to achieve the finish you want. For example, you may need to start with a coarse disc to remove an old surface finish, followed by medium and then fine discs to create a perfectly smooth surface.

Using a finishing sander

This sander scrubs the surface of the wood, moving its baseplate in small orbits to give a very fine, scratch-free surface finish. Large models take third-sheets (230 x 93mm) of abrasive paper; smaller models called palm sanders take quarter-sheets (115 x 70mm) or special own-brand shaped sheets. Those with a dust extraction facility use perforated sanding sheets, often attached with touch-and-close (Velcro) fastenings. Make sure the sheets you buy will fit your sander.

1 Select the correct grade of abrasive sheet for the finish you want to achieve, and attach it to the sanding pad so that the holes in sheet and pad are aligned. Press it firmly into place on the pad.

2 Connect the sander to the hose of your vacuum cleaner using the adaptor provided, and switch the vacuum cleaner on. Or fit the dust bag if the tool has one.

3 Hold the tool against the surface you want to sand and switch on the power. Keep the sander moving backwards and forwards over the surface until it is smooth.

Using a belt sander

A belt sander is ideal for fast removal of material – for example, smoothing rough-sawn timber in the garden – and it will also strip paint and sand other materials such as plastic or metal if fitted with the appropriate abrasive belt. Note that there are more than a dozen different belt sizes available to fit different belt sander makes and models, so make sure you buy the correct size for your machine.

1 Release the roller tension lever and fit the belt over the rollers. Check that it is aligned with the edges of the rollers and tension the belt. Also check the tracking adjustment to ensure that the belt is positioned correctly. If it is not, it will run off the rollers in use.

2 Fit the dust bag or connect the sander to your vacuum cleaner hose via the adaptor supplied.

3 Switch the sander on and drive it over the surface you are sanding, working only along the grain direction. Keep the tool moving, or you will gouge out more material than necessary and leave an uneven finish. Change to finer grades of belt to achieve the finish you want.

Using a detail sander

This small orbital sander uses triangular sanding sheets attached to a matching pad, and is used for sanding into corners where an orbital sander will not reach. It does not usually have a dust bag. Some models have a rotating head that allows you to use all three corners of the sheet before replacing it; on fixed-head machines you reposition the abrasive sheet.

Using wood filler

The type of wood filler you choose depends on whether the wood is going to be painted or simply waxed or varnished.

Wood must have a well-prepared surface before the final finish is applied. This means filling any holes before the wood is finally sanded smooth. If the wood is to be left its natural colour, buy a wood filler that matches. If it is going to be painted, fill with an interior filler.

Tools *Filling knife; abrasive paper; electric sander.*

Materials *Interior filler or wood filler.*

1 If you plan to paint the wood, use a power sander with fine abrasive paper to key existing paintwork. Then wash it with a solution of hot water and sugar soap.

2 If you are repainting the area, use interior wood filler to fill any defects such as cracks or dents. Be sure to press the filler in firmly and scrape away any excess.

3 Once the filler has set hard, sand it smooth ready for painting.

4 If you intend to apply a finish through which the wood can be seen – stain, wax or varnish – then sand it smooth and fill it with a wood filler (known as stopping) that matches the colour of the bare wood as closely as possible.

5 Press the stopping into the holes and cracks, taking care not to spread it into the surrounding grain.

6 Wait until the stopping has dried to the same colour all over – usually about 30 minutes – then sand it flat.

Filling an open woodgrain

If a wooden door has a very open grain, and you want to achieve a smooth painted finish, you will need to work in a paste of fine-surface filler. Apply the filler with a flexible filling knife, pushing it right into the grain. Then wipe away the excess with a damp rag.

Painting woodwork

To avoid a disappointing finish, you should sand wood smooth and fill any holes before painting. Bare wood also needs a sealing coat of primer.

Tools *Paintbrushes; abrasive paper; wood sanding block; thin piece of wood; dusting brush; lint-free cloth or tack rag.*

Materials *Filler for wood painted indoors; knotting; primer; undercoat; topcoat.*

1 Brush a coat of knotting over any resinous areas or knots in the wood so they are sealed and resin cannot seep through.

2 Apply an even coat of primer to bare wood and leave it to dry.

3 Use fine grade abrasive paper wrapped around a block of wood to rub lightly over primed areas to remove any rough bits.

4 Remember to sand moulded areas as well. Use abrasive paper round a thin piece of wood, or a flexible sander.

5 Put one undercoat on light surfaces and two on dark ones. Use an undercoat appropriate to the colour of the paint.

6 When the undercoat is dry, gently rub with abrasive paper. Remove dust with a dusting brush. To pick up remaining dust, wipe with a damp lint-free cloth (a clean old handkerchief is ideal) or a tack rag impregnated with resins that remove dust.

7 Apply the topcoat with a brush that is an appropriate size for the surface.

Varnishing woodwork

If you leave woodwork bare, it will become marked and stained over time. Varnish will protect the surface as well as bringing out the wood's natural colour and showing its grain.

Tools *Paint kettle; measuring jug; rubber gloves; paintbrushes; fine wet-and-dry sanding sponge; tack cloth; 0000-grade wire wool; duster.*

Materials *Varnish; white spirit; wax polish.*

Before you start Consider which type of varnish you want to use. The two main choices are acrylic and polyurethane. Acrylic is quick drying and odour-free; polyurethane is harder wearing but smells strongly when you apply it.

1 For best results, thin the varnish before you apply the first coat (there is no need to thin varnish for the second coat). Measure a small quantity of varnish into a measuring jug, note the volume, and pour it into the paint kettle. Next, measure about a tenth of this volume in water (if you are using acrylic varnish) or white spirit (for polyurethane) and add the water or white spirit to the varnish. Stir thoroughly. Wash out the measuring jug immediately.

2 Fold the lint-free cloth into a ball, dip it into the diluted varnish and wipe it along the grain of the wood in smooth, parallel bands. Wear rubber gloves, as this is a messy job. Discard the cloth afterwards.

CHECK THE TINT FIRST

Using a tinted varnish rather than a clear one will add colour without permanently staining the wood. There are wood shades and paintbox colours available. Before you start, test the tint of the varnish by painting patches of one, two and three coats of varnish on a piece of spare wood. If the tinted varnish is slightly too dark, add a little water to acrylic varnish or white spirit to polyurethane, and then paint more patches to see if the colour has lightened sufficiently.

3 When the first coat is dry, sand the surface lightly with a fine sanding sponge, to 'key' the surface for the next coat.

4 Wipe away all the dust with a tack cloth. If you can't find one in your DIY shop, you can make one by dipping a lint-free cloth in white spirit.

5 Brush on the second coat of varnish as soon as possible, before dust has a chance to settle back onto the surface. Apply the varnish along the grain, then brush across the grain to make sure the bands have blended. Finish off with light brush strokes along the grain.

6 It is almost impossible to achieve a perfect finish. Once the varnish has set hard, feel for any blemishes with your fingertips and rub them gently with a pad of fine wire wool dipped in wax polish.

HELPFUL TIPS

• If you need to fill wood that is to be varnished, buy a wood filler that will match the colour of the finish. Fillers are made in a limited colour range, so look at the filler colour chart in the shop and choose the nearest. If you can, take a piece of the wood with you. Do not match the wood against wet filler; it will become paler as it dries.

• To avoid creating bubbles in the varnish, don't scrape the loaded brush against the rim of the tin or across a string tied across a paint kettle; instead, just load your brush and then tap the sides of the container with the brush. The excess varnish will drip off the brush.

• If the wood looks too shiny after varnishing, you can reduce the sheen with fine wire wool. Rub gently, with the grain, to cut back the gloss so that there is hardly any reflection at all. This is particularly suitable for pale woods.

• Commercial dip-stripping in hot caustic soda is a quick and easy way to remove layers of paint from moulded doors and leave a bare wood finish suitable for varnishing. Not all doors are worth stripping, so test one before paying for a whole set; also, joints may become loose and doors may warp, so check with the company that your doors are suitable. Mark each door with a chiselled Roman numeral in the top edge to keep a note of which door belongs with which frame.

Using waxes and oil finishes

Wax and oil finishes are most often used on furniture and wood with a natural finish, where the grain of the wood is visible. Oil finishes are best suited to wood that will be subjected to moisture and frequent handling. Wax is easier to apply but the surface must be completely smooth and clean before application. For tips on using finishes on wood furniture see pages 120–124.

Applying an oil finish

Tools *Plastic cups; foam brushes; clean lint-free rags; abrasive paper; latex gloves.*
Materials *Oil finish.*

Before you start Spread out plenty of newspaper in the work area. Most oil finishes are non-toxic but wear latex gloves and dispose of used rags and brushes in an airtight container as they can spontaneously combust if left crumpled in a ball.

1 Strip off any old finish and sand the wood until smooth. Start with 80 grit paper, then 120, and finally finish with 180 grit paper, sanding in the direction of the grain to remove any scratch marks.

2 Dust off then wipe down the surface with a tack rag or a cloth, which has been sprinkled with a little linseed oil. Turn the cloth often to expose a clean surface.

3 Use a foam brush to apply a coat of oil in the direction of the grain. Avoid over brushing and do not stop halfway through the job or a line will appear in the finish.

4 After 15 minutes use a clean rag to wipe any excess oil from the surface. When one rag becomes saturated replace it with a clean one.

5 Leave the oil to soak in for 3 hours then apply a second coat and wipe down as before.

6 Leave for 24 hours and then use a soft clean cloth to buff to a smooth shine.

HELPFUL TIP

Waxes and oils will alter the colour of the wood, so test them on a scrap piece of wood or on an area which will not be visible before you start the job.

Applying a wax finish

Tools *Abrasive paper; soft cloths; latex gloves.*

Materials *Wax; acetone or denatured alcohol.*

1 Strip off any previous finishes and sand the surface smooth. Make sure that you remove any surface imperfections and scratches that will show through the finish.

2 Wipe down the surface with acetone or denatured alcohol to remove any residual surface impurities.

3 Immediately rub on the wax, as detailed in the manufacturer's instructions. Be careful not to apply too much; two thin coats are better than one thick one.

4 Use a soft lint-free cloth and buff to a smooth shine until all the wax has penetrated into the surface of the wood.

Woodworking
projects

Choosing wall fixings

If you are fixing a weightbearing unit to a wall – for example, shelving – it is always essential to provide good, strong fittings, suitable for the load.

Fixings for solid walls

For masonry walls Use screws that will penetrate the wall by a minimum of 50mm, driven into plastic wall plugs that match the screw gauge.

On timber-framed walls Where the screws pass directly into the framing, 40mm penetration will be adequate, unless a heavy load is to be put on the shelves, when screws should go in by 50mm. Before putting up any fixing, always use a battery-powered cable detector to locate cables or pipes buried in walls.

STANDARD WALL PLUGS

Finned plastic Tapered plug with split end to allow expansion, and either fins or lugs to prevent it turning in the hole. A rim of flexible ears prevent it being pushed in too far. Each size will accept screws of several lengths and gauges.

Ribbed plastic Has no fins or lugs, but the shallow lengthways ribs prevent it from turning in the hole. Sold in colour-coded sizes.

Strip plastic Straight-sided plug with shallow lengthways ribs. Can be bought in strips and cut to length with a trimming knife.

Masonry nail Hardened galvanised nail that will penetrate and grip when driven into bricks or blocks. Not suitable for use in concrete or hard stone. Lengths typically from 15 to 100mm.

A fast way of fixing timber battens to brick walls. Choose a length that will penetrate beyond the fixing by about 15mm into bare masonry or about 25mm into a plastered wall. Hammer with short, positive strokes. Nails will not bend, and will shatter if not struck squarely. Wear eye protection.

Woodscrew and wall plug The fibre or plastic plug expands to fit the hole and grip the masonry wall. Plugs are in lengths from 15 to 90mm.

For lightweight fittings, use No. 8 gauge screws and matched plugs. For heavier fittings use No. 10 or No. 12 gauge screws. The screw should be long enough to extend about 25mm into the masonry after passing through the fitting and the plaster.

Hammer-in fixing or nail plug A screw with a special thread for easy driving, ready-fitted into a nylon sleeve. It can be tapped with a hammer into a drilled hole. Lengths typically 50 to 160mm will fix objects from about 5 to 110mm thick.

A strong, fast method for fixing a lot of timber battens to brick or concrete. Also suitable for lightweight fixings into building blocks. The hole should extend 5–15mm beyond the screw tip. So for a screw 50mm long fixing a 10mm thick object, make wall holes at least 45mm deep.

Frame fixing A long screw ready-fitted into a nylon wall plug. Drill the hole through the frame into the wall, push or lightly tap the fixing through and tighten with a screwdriver. Lengths to secure frames from about 20 to 110mm thick. A secure and convenient method of fixing new or replacement door or window frames to walls. Useful for repairing a door frame that has worked loose. As a guide, the depth of the masonry hole should be at least five times the diameter of the plug.

Fixings for hollow walls, ceilings and lightweight blocks

Woodscrew and plug The screw has a winged plastic plug that spreads out to grip the back of a wall or ceiling board. The plug can be re-used if the screw is withdrawn. For lightweight or medium fittings to plasterboard, hardboard or plywood (including hollow doors) up to about 25mm thick. The cavity behind the board needs to be at least 15mm deep.

Machine screw and expanding rubber plug The screw fits into a nut in a rubber sleeve that is compressed to grip the back of the board. The plug stays in place if the screw is withdrawn. Plugs are sold with or without a screw. A strong fixing for plasterboard, plywood, hardboard, sheet metal, glass or plastic, up to about 45mm thick. The plug protects the screw from vibration and rusting. It can also be used as a wall plug in masonry where it shapes to the hole's contours.

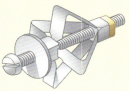

Machine screw and metal cavity fixing A metal plug with a nut welded in the end. It collapses to form metal wings that grip the back of the board. A strong fixing for heavyweight fixtures to hardboard, plasterboard, chipboard, plywood and fibreboard, up to about 35mm thick.

Gravity toggle A machine screw with a swinging metal bar (toggle) attached. When the screw is inserted, the toggle swings down and grips the back of the wall. It is lost if the screw is withdrawn.

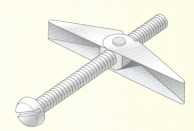

A strong fixing for plasterboard or lath-and-plaster walls. The cavity has to be at least 32mm wide, or wider for larger sizes.

Spring toggle A machine screw fitted with a spring-operated toggle bar that folds back while it is being inserted and then springs open when it is inside the cavity. The toggle is lost if the screw is withdrawn. Typical size range is for screws 50–80mm long.

A strong fixing for plasterboard or lath-and-plaster walls and ceilings. The cavity has to be at least 45mm wide – even wider for larger sizes. The toggle can be used with a hook for hanging a light-fitting from the ceiling.

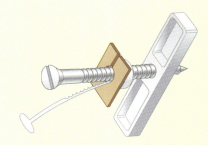

Nylon toggle and collar A nylon collar that takes a wood screw and is linked by a notched nylon strip to a toggle. After insertion, the strip is used to draw the toggle towards the collar to take the screw tip and grip the back of the board. It is then cut off. Typical size is for No. 6 woodscrews. The collar closes the drilled hole and the adjustable fitting is used for fixing to plasterboard, lath-and-plaster or suspended ceilings of different thicknesses. The toggle is retained if the screw is withdrawn.

SHELF MATERIALS

White melamine-coated chipboard

Coloured melamine-coated chipboard

Heavyweight melamine-veneered chipboard

MDF clear varnished

Coated chipboard
Inexpensive and needs no finishing. Choose 15mm board for light items and 18mm for heavier loads, such as books.

Medium-density fibreboard (MDF)
Versatile and easy to work with but must be sealed or painted. It is relatively inexpensive. It is sold in sheets and comes in several thicknesses.

Softwood (pine) stained and polished

Wood-veneered chipboard

Plywood, coated with varnish

Hardwood (oak) polished

Timber and wood-veneered chipboard
More expensive than coated chipboard and needs to be sealed, with varnish or paint, for example.

See also pages 17–19.

Choosing shelving

Shelves can be put up just about anywhere – alcoves are a good choice, but any wall space can be used. There is a huge selection to choose from, ranging from flat-pack units or tailor made shelving.

Floating shelves These are so-named because they have no visible means of support. They look modern, clean and attractive, and are great for display purposes. However, they are suitable only for light items. Floating shelves are available in kit form and are supported by a concealed batten or rods fixed into the wall.

CHOOSING FIXED BRACKETS

Most right-angle brackets have one arm longer than the other. Fix the long arm to the wall, unless the instructions state otherwise. The width of a shelf should be only about 25mm greater than the length of the horizontal arm of the bracket. Large overhangs can lead to the shelf becoming overloaded, which may cause the brackets to fail. Always secure shelves by screwing them to the brackets.

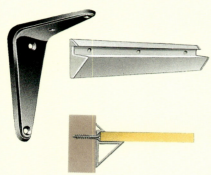

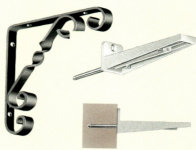

For heavy loads
• Usually made in high-strength pressed steel. One type has a continuous aluminium bracket that supports the shelf along its whole length.
• Sizes range from 75 x 50mm to 350 x 350mm. Aluminium strip comes in lengths from 600mm to 2.5m.
• Finishes include: red, black, brown and white epoxy-coated; or galvanised (silvery).
• The manufacturers usually state load capacity on packaging.

For medium/heavy loads
A range of styles for different types of medium to heavy loads. Includes wrought-iron, pressed steel, both with holes for screws, and plastic with a steel pin support (for a radiator shelf).
• Sizes range from 100 x 75mm to 240 x 240mm.
• Finishes include: red, brown, gold, yellow, green, black and silver. Radiator shelf support is in white or brown plastic.

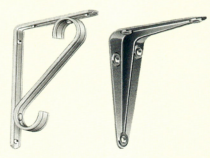

For medium/light loads
Suitable for narrow shelves where other brackets are too large. Designed for reinforcing the corners of cabinets, but suitable for shelves. Radiator shelf option wedges behind radiator and needs no wall fixings.
• Sizes: 50 x 50mm; and a radiator shelf of 125 or 150mm.
• Finishes include: cadmium-plated and galvanised (silvery).

For light loads
Made in either pressed steel or aluminium, they have holes for screws.
• Sizes from 100 x 75mm to 300 x 250mm.
• Finishes include: black or grey dip painted and anodised silver, gold and white for braced bracket.

Utility shelving for sheds and garages
Medium weight, for supporting one or two shelves at a time.
• Sizes from 240 x 165mm to 310mm wide by 280mm deep (double bracket).
• Finished in epoxy-coated orange only.

BRACKET INTERVALS

Buying the cheapest shelf-and-bracket system can be a false economy if you plan to fill the shelves with heavy loads, such as books. The cheapest shelving material is the weakest, and if it is to be loaded up it will require closer support. This table is a guide to the intervals at which typical shelf materials need to be supported.

15mm chipboard (coated or plain); **15mm softwood (finished thickness)**	Heavy loads 400mm Medium loads 600mm
18mm coated chipboard; 18mm MDF; **18mm softwood; 18mm hardwood**	Heavy loads 500mm Medium loads 700mm
25mm MDF; 25mm softwood; **18mm plywood; 22mm hardwood**	Heavy loads 700mm Medium loads 900mm
32mm veneered chipboard; **32mm softwood; 25mm plywood;** **25mm hardwood**	All loads 900mm

Strengthening shelves with battens and lipping

Shelves can be reinforced to improve their resistance to bending. The reinforcements can also be a decorative feature, hiding fixings or strip lights.

Apply a softwood or hardwood batten – a thick piece of wood – to the front or back edge of the shelf. It should run the full length and can be on the top or bottom. For extra strength, battens can be fixed to both front and back edges. The deeper the batten, the greater the strength. Fix the battens to the shelf with glue and screws, screwing through the shelf.

Hardwood lipping – a thin strip of wood – can be glued and pinned along the front edge. It may be the same depth as the shelf to give a decorative finish only, or it may be much deeper, which will strengthen as well as decorate.

POSITIONING THE BRACKETS

End supports Maximum bending occurs under heavy loads.

Supports set in Loads at each end balance the central load.

The bracket positions can give shelves greater resistance to bending. If the shelves extend beyond the brackets they are less likely to bend in the middle. But they must be fixed to the brackets with screws, otherwise they will tip up if a weight is placed at one end – when putting up the first pile of books, for example.

Thick battens or thin hardwood lipping
These reinforce a shelf and can also be decorative. Keep in mind that lipping that extends under the front edge will slightly restrict the height of the items you can store on the shelf below.

A spirit level has one or more clear vials filled with a liquid. When the level is truly horizontal, a bubble in the liquid floats within an area marked on the centre vial to indicate that it is exactly level.

Laser level

State-of-the-art laser levels fire a laser beam enabling horizontal or vertical guidelines to be marked quickly and accurately.

Laser levels have a wide range of uses including guaranteeing a consistent and accurate level for wall lights across a room or positioning brackets for shelves within an alcove. However, their strongest benefit is in establishing levels for setting out outdoor work, such as putting up fences or laying paving.

Using a plumb line

A plumb line is simply a weight tied to a length of string. If you hold it firmly at the top, it will hang vertically, provided that the string and weight are not touching anything. You can buy a plumb line, or make your own by tying a heavy nut to the end of a length of string.

Tools *Plumb line; a hardback book; a long screw; pencil; a long straightedge, such as a length of track from a shelving system.*

Load test Before fixing a shelf in place, check whether it will bow under the weight you intend to put on it. Rest the shelf on bricks set at the proposed bracket spacing, load it up and lay a straightedge along its surface. If the shelf bows, either move the bricks (and consequently the brackets) closer together, or increase the thickness of the shelf material.

Finding your levels

When you are putting up shelves, the most important part of the job is getting the shelves horizontal and the brackets vertical.

Spirit level

Investing in a good spirit level is crucial. Levels are available in different lengths and designs, from miniature and pocket levels to long carpenter's levels and even digital levels that give a readout of a slope angle.

1 When fixing shelving track, mark and then drill the hole for the topmost fixing screw.

2 Plug the hole and partly drive a long screw into it.

3 Suspend the plumb line from the screw so that it hangs as close to the floor as possible.

4 Let the string become steady. Then place one edge of the book on the wall and slide it up to the string until they touch. Mark the wall where the corner of the book has come to rest.

5 Remove the book, string and screw. Using a track from the shelving system or a straight wooden batten, draw a line between the centre of the screw hole and the pencil mark. This line will be the centre line for the track or brackets to be fitted.

6 Other vertical lines on the wall can be measured from the first line, using a steel tape measure.

Putting up a fixed shelf

Whether for storage or display, fixed shelves must be sturdy, spacious and perfectly level.

Tools *Pencil; spirit level; drill; masonry or wood bit to fit wall plugs; screwdriver. Possibly a straight wooden batten.*

Materials *Brackets; screws for fixing brackets to wall; wall plugs to fit screws; shelf; small screws for fixing shelf to brackets.*

Before you start Check the walls with a battery-powered pipe and wire detector so as not to drill through any hidden pipes or cables. Use it to detect the positions of the studs on a timber-framed wall.

1 Hold a spirit level against the wall at the point where you want the shelf. Check that it is level and draw a light pencil line on the wall. For a long shelf, rest the spirit level on a straight wooden batten.

2 Hold one bracket against the wall with the top against the mark. Use the spirit level to check that it is vertical, and then mark the wall through the screw holes with the pencil.

3 Repeat for the second bracket. If there are more than two brackets, it is best to fix the outside ones to the wall, and then tie a piece of string tightly between them across the tops. Then the intermediate brackets can be lined up exactly.

4 Drill holes about 45mm into the wall. Use a masonry bit (or a twist bit for wooden studs).

5 Insert plugs into masonry, and screw the brackets tightly to the wall. If the plug turns in the wall as you drive in the screw, remove it, insert a larger one and try again. Do not use plugs in wood.

6 Lay the shelf across the brackets. Using a pencil or bradawl, mark the underside of the shelf through the bracket holes.

7 Drill pilot holes for the small screws and screw the shelf into position.

HELPFUL TIPS

• Right-angled brackets will need screws about 45mm long to fix them to the wall. The screw must go through the plaster and at least 25mm into the brickwork, or into the wood stud if it is a stud partition wall.
• Don't use winged wall plugs to fix brackets to thin hollow walls unless the shelf is only to be used to hold a light decorative object.
• The screws should be the heaviest gauge that the holes in the bracket will take – usually No. 8 gauge on small ones and No. 10 or 12 on larger ones.

Shelves in alcoves

An ideal place to fit shelves is in an alcove beside a chimney breast. This is best done using wooden battens cut and screwed to the side and rear walls of the alcove.

Positioning the battens

Tools *Tape measure; pencil; steel ruler; tenon saw; mitre box; spirit level; power drill; twist drill bits; masonry bits; countersink bit; screwdriver.*

Materials *Wood for battens 50 x 25mm; timber or MDF shelves cut to fit alcove; 63mm No. 8 screws and wall plugs; wood filler.*

Before you start Cut battens to the length of the back wall and shorter ones to the depth of each shelf. Drill and countersink screw holes no more than 300mm apart through each batten. To make battens less noticeable the ends can be angled or curved. If the walls of the alcove are uneven see page 66.

1 Mark the position of each shelf, checking that the spacing between them is large enough for the items you want to store there – don't forget to allow for the thickness of the shelving material, too.

2 Hold the rear batten to the mark with a spirit level on top. Mark the wall through one end hole with the twist bit. Switch to a masonry bit and drill and plug the hole. Drive in a screw part way.

HELPFUL TIPS

• Gaps around shelves in an alcove can be hidden by pinning strips of quadrant beading over them.
• You can also strengthen the shelves, and conceal brackets and any gaps at the ends of the shelves, by gluing and pinning a narrow strip of wood along the front edges (see page 62), although this will slightly reduce the height of the space below.

3 Hold the rear batten level and mark the other holes in the same way. Allow the batten to drop out of the way when you drill the wall, then plug the holes and drive the other screws.

4 Position the first side batten, ensuring that it is level with the rear one. Mark the wall beneath it as a guide. Mark drill holes in the same way as for the rear batten. Repeat for the other side batten.

5 Screw the side battens into position. You will be able to hide the countersunk screw heads with wood filler.

Fitting the shelves

Before you start Few walls are true, and your alcove is unlikely to have perfect right angles. To assess the 'squareness' of the alcove, use a try square (or a triangular offcut from the corner of a sheet of board) to see if the two side walls are at right angles to the back one. Then hold a plumb line at ceiling level to see whether the walls are vertical.

1 If the alcove tapers, measure the precise width of the back wall of the alcove using an adjustable bevel, then mark the same measurement on the back of the shelf. Set the adjustable bevel to one internal corner of the alcove and use it to mark a cutting line across one end of the shelf. Repeat for the other corner. If there are any gaps, see tip left.

Alternatively Use two sheets of card if you don't have an adjustable bevel. Butt the edge of one sheet against the back wall of the alcove and lay the other piece on top so that it butts against the side wall.

Tape the sheets together and mark one shelf end. Repeat for the other corner.

2 After you have cut a shelf to fit, drill and countersink a couple of holes through each end and use woodscrews to secure the shelves to the battens.

HELPFUL TIPS

• Instead of fixing battens straight to the walls of an alcove, you can fix vertical side panels and suspend the shelves from these. Side panels must be at right angles to the back wall. They must also be vertical and parallel to one another.
• If the walls are not flat, square or upright, the side panels will have to be mounted on spacer battens.
• Gaps between the walls and the side panels can be concealed with timber strips, scribed to the shape of the wall and pinned into place.

Built-in cupboards

Alcoves are perfect for built-in cupboards. The sides and back of the alcove act as a ready-made support for shelves and you can simply add a framework at the front for some doors.

First measure the width of the alcove and select the doors. Doors come in standard sizes, and you may be lucky enough to find some that suit your alcove perfectly. If not, you will have to modify the framework and possibly alter the door dimensions slightly.

Assessing the squareness of the alcove

The side and back walls of your alcove should be flat and square to each other, but this may not be the case. (To check this see Fitting the shelves, opposite.) If the squares and verticals are a little awry, you can correct any problems as you build the unit by inserting packing between the woodwork and the walls.

Planning the structure

The cupboard needs a top, some wall battens, and a front frame fixed to the walls and the floor to support the doors. Any intermediate shelves will be supported by the side walls of the alcove.
　　Choose the thickness of the framing timbers to suit your door sizes; anything from 25 to 75mm thick is suitable. By using surface-mounted flush hinges, you can then adjust the door positions on the frame to help make up any discrepancy between the door and alcove widths. If you need to alter the door widths to fit your alcove, you can saw or plane off up to 25mm from each vertical edge; the amount depends on whether the doors are solid or panelled.

Building up the framework

Tools *Tape measure; pencil; try square; tenon saw; mitre box; power drill; twist drill bits; masonry drill bit; countersink bit; spirit level; shape tracer; coping saw; screwdriver; panel saw or power saw; bradawl.*

Materials *Off-the-shelf cupboard doors; 9mm MDF for shelves; 50 x 25mm planed softwood for shelf supports; 50 x 50mm planed softwood for front frame; glass-paper or abrasive sanding block; wall plugs; 63 and 75mm No. 8 countersunk screws; PVA woodworking adhesive; panel pins; surface-mounted flush hinges plus fixing screws (usually supplied with the hinges); door handles; decorator's mastic.*

The framework consists of horizontal shelf support battens fixed to the alcove walls, a vertical batten at each side to which the doors will be hinged, and a horizontal batten at the top and bottom to complete the front frame. If the alcove is more than about 750mm wide, add a central vertical brace to stiffen the frame. The height of the frame should be about 50mm more than the height of the doors you have chosen. The depth depends on whether you want the cupboard to finish flush with the face of the chimney breast, or to be recessed slightly. If you need to reduce the width of over-size doors, do it before you start building the cupboard. You can generally remove up to 25mm from each side, depending on the style of door.

3 Measure the width of the alcove at floor level (between the skirting boards) and cut the bottom frame member to size. Screw it to the floor so its inner face is vertically below the ends of the wall battens.

1 Mark a line on the alcove walls where you want the top of the cupboard and the middle shelf to be. Fix three 50 x 25mm battens to the back and side walls of the alcove (see page 66) to support the middle shelf. Use a spirit level to check that they are perfectly level.

2 Fix three more wall battens in the same way to support the top of the cupboard. Make sure that all the side battens are the same length, as the front frame will butt up against their outer ends.

4 Take measurements for the top and bottom shelves (see page 66 again for details about matching uneven side walls) and cut them to size. Lay the bottom shelf in place on the lower wall battens.

HELPFUL TIP

Paint, varnish or stain the shelves and the front frame before you add the doors. If there are any slight gaps between the shelves or the frame and the alcove walls, fill them with decorator's mastic first.

5 Fix two vertical battens to the walls to form the sides of the front frame. Each should be long enough to finish level with the top of the upper set of wall battens. Use a shape tracer to copy the profile of the skirting board, transfer it to the batten and use a coping saw to cut a matching notch at the bottom end of each batten so it will fit round the skirting board.

7 Use woodworking adhesive to glue the top of the cupboard to the wall battens and the top of the front frame.

8 Make pilot holes for the hinge screws with a bradawl and fix the hinges to the rear faces of the doors, about 75mm from their top and bottom edges. Offer the doors up to the frame and mark where each hinged edge will be positioned on the side frames, allowing for 2-3mm clearance between the closed doors.

9 Screw the hinges on each door to the frame. Check that the doors are aligned and close without touching each other. Add handles to complete the job (see below).

6 Measure the width of the alcove at the level of the upper wall battens and cut the top frame member to this measurement. In a wide alcove, cut another vertical batten for the central brace, to provide extra support for the front frame. Screw the horizontal batten to the tops of the vertical wall battens and the brace to complete the front frame.

Self-assembly fixings for flat-pack furniture

When you buy an item of flat-pack furniture, it comes with fixing holes already drilled and special types of fixing to enable you to assemble it yourself easily and with the minimum number of tools. Here are some of the most common fixings that you are likely to encounter.

Many fixings are also available to buy separately so that you can use them when making your own units. Always use fittings in pairs and use a steel ruler, not a tape measure, when marking where to drill – it is essential for drill holes to be accurately positioned if the unit is to be square when assembled. You won't need many tools to assemble flat-pack furnitures – often all that's necessary is a special spanner or hex key supplied with the unit.

Two block fitting (Lok joint)

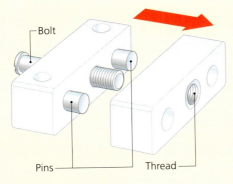

The joint consists of two plastic blocks and is normally used to join two sections of cupboard together such as a side to the base. One of the blocks is screwed to the base and the other to the side into pre-drilled holes; a bolt is then screwed in to hold the two sections firmly together. One of the advantages of this type of fixing is that it can be disassembled and reassembled whenever necessary with no loss of strength.

Plastic corner block

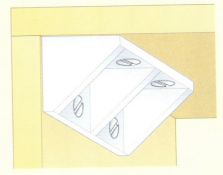

One of the simplest of the fittings that is often found in flat pack furniture. Plastic corner blocks hold two panels together at a perfect right angle. As screws are driven into the carcase material, this fitting cannot be taken apart and reused without compromising its strength.

Dowels

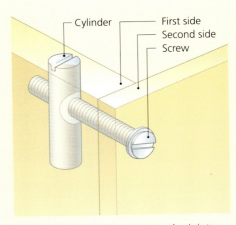

Dowels are for more permanent joints and those that are not to be taken apart once assembled. Usually about 25–30mm long, they are glued in place. Like the majority of the fixings used in flat pack furniture they are tapped into factory-made pre-drilled holes. Although simple they are very effective and give a strong concealed joint.

Dowel and screw fitting

These are one of the most popular joints used in flat pack furniture. The cylinder is inserted into a factory-made pre-drilled hole in one side of the cabinet. A machine screw is then inserted into a hole in the other side until it meets the cylinder. The two components are tightened with a screwdriver until both sides of the cabinet

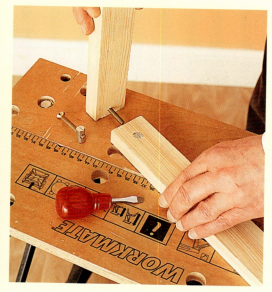

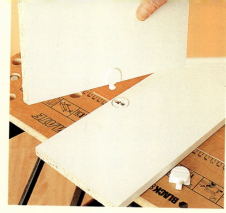

Some cam fittings come with the peg attached to a disc the same size as the cam. Both components slot into pre-drilled holes in the panels to be joined.

pull together. The slot in the head of the cylinder part of the fitting allows you to align it so that it will receive the screw (above). Although it is possible to over-tighten these fittings they do hold very securely and can be repeatedly taken apart with no loss of strength.

Cam lock fittings

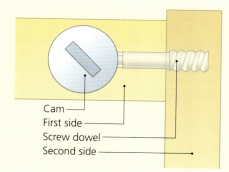

Cam
First side
Screw dowel
Second side

Like the dowel and screw fitting, this fastening is for joining two planks or panels together. The cam is dropped into a shallow recess on the face of one part and a screw with a pronounced head or a steel screw dowel is driven into a pre-drilled hole in the other part to be joined.

The head of the screw passes through a clearance hole in the first part and into the cam. Turning the cam 90° clockwise tightens the joint.

Another variation on this type of fitting replaces the peg with a special moulding like a wall plug. This is pushed into a hole drilled in the edge of the second board. A pin is driven into the plug and the fitting is assembled as before.

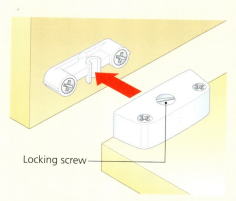

Locking screw

This cam fitting is similar to the Lok joint. The two parts of the joint are screwed into separate panels. The two panels are then brought together and the screw is turned through 90° to lock the joint.

Dowel and bush fitting

This fitting consists of a zinc alloy bush and a steel dowel. Screw the dowel into the face of one board so that when it is butt-jointed with the second board it will align with the hole drilled in the second board's edge. The dowel reaches the bush through that hole and is locked in place by turning the grub screw in the bush.

Housing and bolt fitting

A bolt screws into the side panel of a cupboard or shelf unit and fits into the housing, which slots into a hole drilled in the underside of the shelf. These fittings are useful for strengthening shelves in an existing unit or for adding extra shelves.

Assembling flat-pack furniture

Whether you are putting together a simple bookshelf or a small bathroom cabinet follow these steps to success.

Most flat-pack units consist of a series of panels that are fitted together to create a basic box. Extras, such as doors, shelves and internal fittings, are then added to this to complete the job. Always work in a logical order, following the instructions that came with the unit.

1 Unpack the kit and lay out all the components, including the assembly fittings and any other items of hardware such as hinges, handles and feet. Lay the panels on a carpet, other soft surface or the box they were supplied in to minimise scratches.

2 Identify all the parts, using the instructions, and check that you have the right number of fixings – there is usually a numbered checklist included with the instructions. If any appear to be missing, look inside the packaging to see if any are loose inside. If you still cannot locate the missing pieces, return the complete unit to the store and ask for a replacement.

3 Start with the base panel, adding any fixed feet first of all. Build tall units, such as bookshelves (see page 75) or wardrobes, on their backs to make the assembly manageable. If the unit has castors or wheels, fit these last or the unit will keep moving about as you try to assemble it.

4 Connect the first side panel to the base panel. The simplest units have pre-drilled holes through which you can drive screws supplied with the furniture (above). Many units use a combination of glued dowels and cam fixings (pages 70–72). In this case, place the dowels and screwed pegs in the base unit and then offer up the side panel. Glue and locate all the dowels in the side panel, then tighten the fixings.

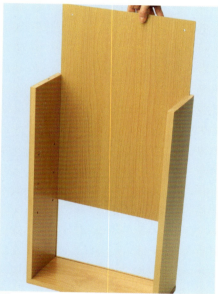

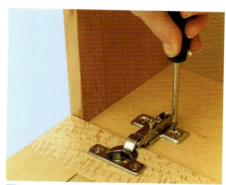

7 Follow the instructions with the unit to add any doors. They will be hung on some form of spring-loaded hinges, and the fitting and fixing holes will all be pre-drilled in the doors and cabinet sides. Fit the hinge body to the door and the mounting plate to the cabinet sides, then connect the two with the short machine screws and adjust them so they hang squarely.

8 Add any shelves, door handles and other internal or external fittings. Double-check that all the assembly fittings are tight, and that you do not have any parts left over.

5 Connect the second side panel to make a three-sided box. If the unit has a back panel, locate this in the grooves in the side panels and slide it into place. Then finish the box by fixing the top panel in position.

6 Many fixings come with cover discs that match the colour of the wood or veneer of the finished item. These make a tidy job of disguising the fixings once the furniture is complete. They can be prised out of their holes if you need access to the fixings to dismantle the furniture.

Customising flat-pack units

There are many ways in which you can modify flat-pack furniture to suit your individual requirements. For example, you can fit drawers into cabinets or you could add extra shelves to storage and display units.

Adding drawers

The simplest and quickest way of adding drawers to storage units and cabinets is to use kit drawers. The cheapest type consists of a set of plastic mouldings that form the drawer sides, and matching plastic support strips which you screw to the inner faces of the cabinet. Grooves in the drawer sides engage on the strips; you must therefore fix these first so you can measure up the drawer width accurately. You may need to provide a hardboard or thin MDF panel for the drawer base.

   More expensive kits consist of two metal drawer sides and matching metal track in which the sides engage to provide a secure sliding mechanism, similar to that found in kitchen base units. You have to provide the drawer base, back and front; you should be able to match the last component to the finish on your flat-pack furniture by choosing melamine-faced chipboard or a piece of softwood cut to size.

1 Fix the tracks inside the cabinet so you can determine the drawer width you need (the instructions give details of the exact measurement allowances required). Use a spirit level to check the tracks are level.

2 Cut the drawer base to size, screw the metal drawer sides to its underside and add the drawer back panel.

3 Fit the adjustable front fixing brackets to the drawer sides, then cut the drawer front to the required size.

4 Centre the drawer assembly on its inner face and mark the positions of the screw fixing holes on it through the fixing brackets. Release the brackets from the drawer sides and screw them to the drawer front. Then clip the front to the drawer sides by engaging the clips in the matching sockets, and tighten the locking screws.

5 Finally add drawer handles if required, and slot the drawer into place on its tracks.

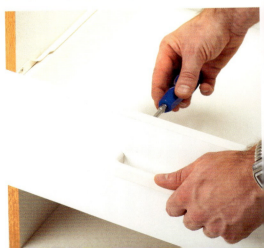

Adding extra shelves

If you want to add fixed shelves to a storage unit or cabinet, you have a choice of fixings – but they will be visible. You can screw through the uprights into the ends of the shelves, or support them on slim wooden battens or plastic corner blocks fixed to the inner face of the uprights. If you prefer adjustable shelves, you have several options.

Push-fit plastic shelf studs The simplest shelf support, these fit into a series of holes drilled in the inner face of each upright. The studs are available in brown and white to match the most common flat-pack furniture finishes, and in clear plastic that is ideal for use with glass shelves. You must measure and mark the hole positions carefully to ensure that the shelves are perfectly horizontal.

Magic wire This allows you to have adjustable shelving with no visible means of support. It is made from 3mm diameter wire, shaped so the ends fit in holes drilled at regular intervals in the sides of the unit. Two wires support each shelf, which needs a groove cut with a circular saw in each end to accept them. Four sizes are available to suit different shelf widths.

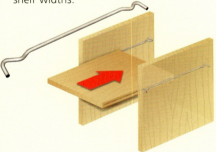

Bookcase strip This allows you to provide infinitely adjustable shelves, and is ideal for use in tall units. The metal strip has slots about 20mm apart into which you clip matching metal clips that support the shelf ends. You need two strips at each side of the unit, positioned about 40mm in from the front and back edges. Choose the surface-mounted type for use in assembled units. It is essential to align the tops of the strips accurately to ensure that the shelves are level when fitted.

Assembling flat-pack shelves

Free-standing shelf units are one of the most popular home storage flat-packs. They are available in a range of heights and widths.

The cheapest and simplest units are utility shelves made from slatted softwood, and are designed for use in a garage or utility room. Shelves made from melamine-faced chipboard, usually with a white or wood-effect finish, are more suited to the living room. Units made from MDF or solid wood are more expensive, but are better at supporting heavy loads such as books or home entertainment equipment, which can soon make chipboard shelves sag.

Assembling a utility shelf unit

Tools *Selection of screwdrivers; perhaps a hammer; perhaps a set of hex (Allen) keys.*

Before you start Unpack everything and check that all the parts and fixings are present. This unit comes with pre-assembled slatted shelves and pre-drilled uprights so all you have to do is attach the shelves to the uprights.

1 Start by screwing one of the four uprights to the top shelf through the pre-drilled holes. Use a try square to check that the upright and shelf are square to each other.

2 Screw the upright to the bottom shelf in the same way. Then fit the second upright.

3 Screw the remaining shelves to the two uprights through the pre-drilled holes. You can drill extra holes to fit the shelves at different levels if you prefer.

4 Turn the shelving unit over and attach the remaining two uprights to the shelves.

5 Stand the unit upright in its chosen position, and secure the top to the wall with a bracket or restraining strap, if required, to prevent it from fallling over.

Building a computer desk

Large items of flat-pack furniture are constructed using special fixings (pages 70–72). Follow the instructions that come with the unit, using these standard techniques to guide you.

Tools *Selection of screwdrivers; perhaps a hammer; perhaps a set of hex (Allen) keys.*

Before you start Unpack the box and lay out all the pieces and fixings. Check them against the instructions and make sure that they are all there and you know which piece is which. Often, a right and left hand piece look almost identical until you check where the fixing holes have been drilled.

1 Insert cam lock screw dowels into predrilled holes according to the instructions.

2 Use your thumb to push the cam locks into the large holes on the opposing panels, making sure that the arrow on the fitting points towards the holes on the raw outside edge of the workpiece. The cam lock pins fit into these holes, so if the locks don't face in the right direction the fixings will not work.

3 Begin to put the piece together in the order specified in the instructions. In this instance the lock pins are screwed into the cam locks using the special key supplied as part of the kit.

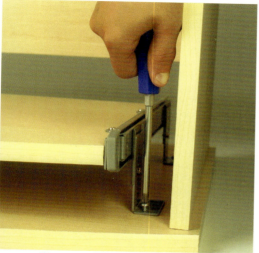

4 This workstation has a sliding keyboard table. The runners for the sliding section are fitted to the keyboard table, and then fixed to the underside of the desk. You will need to turn the desk upside down to make the fixings.

WHEN GLUING IS BEST

If you know that you will not be taking the furniture apart again at some time in the future, consider using adhesive on wood-to-wood joints for a sturdier finished piece. Ordinary white carpenters' PVA adhesive is ideal. Use a damp rag to wipe off any excess adhesive that squeezes from the joints.

5 Make up the shelf section that sits on top of the desk. This fits onto dowels that have been tapped into the desktop with a hammer. Fit the top to the base and push them together to ensure all the dowels have engaged. If you need to, hammer from above, being sure to protect the workpiece with some scrap timber.

6 Finish the item by adding any accessories. In this instance a simple plastic rack for CDs slots into the narrow stack to the left of the desk.

Wood mouldings

Mouldings are practical as well as decorative. Skirting boards save the base of walls from hard knocks. Dado rails are traditionally fixed at a height to protect walls from chair backs. Picture rails, fixed at or above the height of door frames, support heavy pictures and mirrors securely without the need for individual wall fixings. Choose mouldings in a style that reflects the overall design of the room.

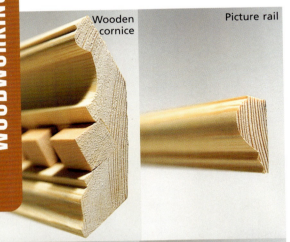

Wooden cornice

Picture rail

Dado rail

Architrave

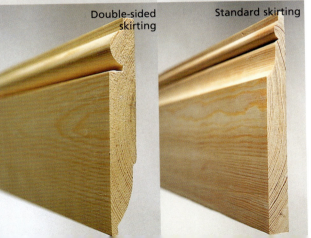

Double-sided skirting

Standard skirting

Most of the wood used in woodworking is square or rectangular in cross section. Mouldings are made by machining wood to create a variety of other cross sections.

Many of these are used for structural jobs as diverse as making windows and doors and forming skirting boards and wall cladding. Other mouldings are purely decorative, being used to edge boards, to cover gaps or to trim and finish items like built-in furniture.

Structural mouldings are generally relatively large in section and machined from softwood, although hardwood versions are available at a price. They include skirting boards, architraves, dado and picture rails, staircase handrails and balusters, windowsills and wall cladding.

Decorative mouldings are machined from hardwoods such as ramin, and include small trim mouldings in quadrant, scotia, half-round and corner profiles.

Embossed trim mouldings are created by impressing decorative designs onto the face of pre-machined mouldings.

MDF mouldings

You can also buy structural mouldings machined from MDF. They have well-finished edges and are free from knots, warping and other defects.

They are often sold primed, ready for the final coat to be applied. Don't use MDF mouldings in bathrooms or kitchens because if they absorb moisture they will swell and distort. Remember to wear a dust mask when cutting or drilling MDF.

Buying mouldings

Measure and list the length of every stretch of wall to which you are going to attach a moulding, then add about 50mm (2in) as a trim allowance for every corner cut required. Visit your timber merchant or DIY store and find out what lengths they have in stock; these usually start at 1.8m and rise in increments of 300mm (12in). Then

choose the mouldings you're going to use and work out a cutting order that involves as little waste as possible.

If you are looking for a replacement moulding, it's a good idea to record its shape before going to a timber merchant. To do this, use profile gauge – a comb-like tool composed of sliding 'needles'. Set the gauge by pressing it against the face of the moulding you want to duplicate.

2 Begin at a corner. Cut the first piece of moulding to length if it runs up to an obstacle such as a door frame and sand down the sawn edge. Mark positions for screw holes at 600mm intervals on the rail. Countersink holes, or the bit may make a ragged hole. Drill the holes with a twist bit.

Fitting picture rails and dados

These timber mouldings will break up high walls. Fix picture rails 450–600mm below ceiling level – they are often level with the top of the door surround. Dado rails were traditionally fitted to protect the wall from chair backs and are now usually positioned at about waist height.

3 Line up the rail with the pencil line, and mark fixing positions on the wall through screw holes. Drill holes in the wall and plug them. Drive one end screw almost all the way in, then the other end screw. Fit the rest of the screws and tighten them all.

Tools *Pencil; straightedge; spirit level; tape measure; tenon saw; abrasive paper; power drill; coping saw; twist, countersink and masonry drill bits; screwdriver; mitre box; portable workbench; filling knife.*

Materials *Mouldings to fit walls; screws and wall plugs; wood filler.*

Before you start Buy only mouldings that are dead straight and have no large knots.

1 To fit the rail, mark a pencil line along the walls at the required height using a straightedge and spirit level or laser level.

GUARD AGAINST INACCURACY

If the floor slopes, do not match the height of a dado or picture rail to it. Either hire a laser level (see page 63), or mark the height of the moulding at one point only, then use the longest spirit level you can obtain to transfer the mark all around the room. Compensate for any slight inaccuracy in the level by turning it end over end as you go.

4 On long walls you will need more than one length of moulding. Avoid a gap opening up over time by cutting the ends that are to meet at a 45° angle. You can use a mitre box to do this (page 8).

Tackling corners

1 A butt joint is the best choice at an internal corner, with the end of one rail scribed and cut to fit against the face of the next section. Draw the shape of the rail on the back of the next length, following the shape of a moulding offcut.

2 Use a coping saw to cut along the marked line. Sand the cut edge and make sure that it fits. Any gaps can be masked later on with wood filler.

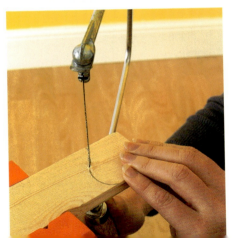

GLUING RAILS IN PLACE

You can fix rails to a wall by applying instant-grip adhesive and holding the moulding in place until the adhesive grips. This takes less time, but the rail cannot then be moved without damaging the plaster.

3 Drill holes in the cut moulding, and drill and plug holes in the wall. Apply woodworking adhesive to the scribed end, place it in position and drive in the fixing screws. Remove extra adhesive with a damp cloth.

4 When taking a rail round an external corner, mitre the joint. Cut the pieces so the joint fits as closely as possible, and glue the angled pieces together as you attach the sections to the wall. If necessary, pin the joint to secure it.

5 Make sure screw heads are countersunk and nail heads are punched well below the surface. Cover the heads with wood filler.

REMOVING A RAIL

Remove an unwanted picture rail or dado by prising it away from its backing using a mallet and an old, wide wood chisel. Start at the centre of the longest length and ease it gently away, working from both edges. Wedge between the backing and the moulding with a scrap of wood or hardboard as soon as possible.

Having removed the rail, make good any holes in the plaster or any other damage. The gap left by the rail can be difficult to disguise if the plaster above and below the rail is at different levels due to the wall having been plastered after the rail was fitted.

Removing and replacing skirting boards

An old wooden skirting board can be levered away from the wall, but this may be difficult if it has been screwed or nailed into the masonry.

Removing a skirting board

Tools *Hammer and bolster chisel; wrecking bar; thin pieces of wood for protecting the wall and for wedging. Possibly also: trimming knife; torch; hacksaw blade; screwdriver.*

Before you start Use a sharp trimming knife to cut through any wallpaper stuck to the top of the skirting board. If the top of the board is covered with plaster, chip it away carefully first.

1 Start levering at an external corner or where skirting butts against a door frame. When removing only part of the skirting, note whether the board to be removed is overlapped by another at an internal corner. If it is, remove the overlapping board first.

2 Ease the skirting board away from the wall using a hammer and bolster chisel, until there is enough space to insert a thin piece of wood, which will protect the wall.

3 Hold the wrecking bar near its hooked end and insert the blade behind the skirting. Prise the board away from the wall, and wedge it with a piece of wood. Move along the skirting board, wedging the board as you go, and continue until the whole board is loosened.

4 When a board is difficult to loosen, wedge a gap open to look behind and check the type of fixing used.

If the fixing is a screw, probe the front of the board to find the head (it will probably be covered with filler). Unscrew it if you can, otherwise cut through it from behind with a hammer and cold chisel or hacksaw blade.

If the fixing is a large cut nail, you can pull the board away, leaving the nail behind. If you cannot prise the nail out, break it off flush with the masonry by bending it from side to side with a series of hammer blows.

Replacing a skirting board

Plaster is rarely taken far down the wall behind skirting.
● When you are fitting new skirting, buy board of the same height as the old to avoid having to patch the plaster. Alternatively, increase the height of the new board by nailing moulding to the top.
● If new skirting board is thinner than the plaster or lining above it, pack behind with an extra piece of timber to bring it out to the required thickness.
● If the plaster does reach to the floor, fix the skirting board through it into the brickwork with screws and wall plugs.

Before you start
• Coat the back of new skirting board with wood preservative to guard against rot.
• Before fitting the new skirting board, lay it flat along the floor and mark on the front the positions of any existing fixing points (see below) so that you can nail through the marks. Fit skirting board to existing fixing points wherever this is possible.

Types of fixing points

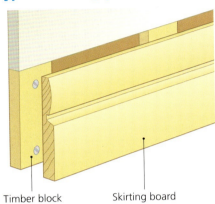

Timber block   Skirting board

The commonest type of fixing point is a timber block. Blocks are nailed or screwed to the wall at 450–600mm intervals.

Fit new blocks if necessary, using timber treated with wood preservative. Fix the blocks with masonry nails or screws and wall plugs.

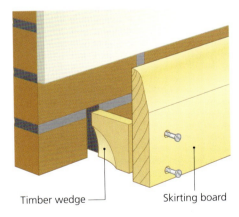

Timber wedge   Skirting board

Another type of fixing point is a timber wedge. These are inserted into the mortar joints between bricks.

If a timber wedge is damaged, remove it by partially driving in a large screw, then pulling it out, together with the wedge, using a crowbar claw or claw hammer. Make and fit a new wedge.

Gluing a skirting board

Modern instant-grip adhesives are so strong that you can secure skirting boards and other mouldings with adhesive instead of using screws or masonry nails.

Apply the adhesive evenly – a zigzag pattern works well – to the back of the moulding. Press firmly against the wall and hold in position with wood offcuts while the adhesive sets. Wipe away any excess adhesive with a damp cloth.

Forming external and internal corners

Before fitting new skirting, shape the ends of the boards where there are external or internal corners.

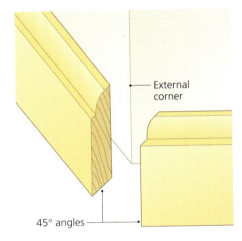

External corner

45° angles

On an external corner, mitre the two boards to meet each other at an angle of 45°. On an internal corner, shape the end of one board to overlap the other, as described below.

1 Fit one board into the internal corner and temporarily nail it in position.

2 Hold the second board butted at right angles to the first and pencil its profile onto the end of the first board.

3 Remove the first board and cut away the end along the pencilled mark with a coping saw.

4 Refit the boards with the second, uncut board pushed into the corner and the first board lapped over it.

Joining straight lengths of skirting board

When joining two straight lengths of skirting board, do not make straight butt joints, which are impossible to hide. Instead, make a scarf joint by cutting the two ends at 45° angles.

Try to position the join where it will not be seen – behind furniture, for instance.

1 Make each joint with matching 45° cuts using a jigsaw with an adjustable sole plate.

2 Fix one length of skirting board in place then position and fix the other. Apply woodworking adhesive to the cut ends and secure the joint with angled pins.

GAPS BELOW THE SKIRTING

A gap of about 5mm between the skirting board and the floor can be very useful if you want to push fitted carpet or vinyl flooring beneath it. But if gaps occur below newly fitted skirting because the floor is not true, the simplest remedy is to nail quadrant or scotia moulding to the bottom of the skirting against the floor.

Do not nail moulding to the floorboards, as these expand and contract more than the skirting, and another gap could open up.

Fixing skirting to a hollow wall

Skirting board fitted to a hollow wall – a partition or a dry-lined wall – is fixed to the vertical studs and the sole plate of the framing. Locate the studs using a pipe and nail detector. Refit the board using 65mm oval nails.

Repairing moulding on a skirting board

It may be impossible to buy matching moulding to repair a damaged section of skirting board (or picture rail) in an old house. You may be able to have a similar moulding cut to order by a timber merchant. Or you can do the job yourself by cutting a matching piece with a router.

Where a small section of ornate moulding is damaged or missing, take an impression from a sound piece by pressing model-casting rubber dental-impression compound against it. Fill this mould with car-body filler. Smooth the cast and glue in place.

The join between two pieces of skirting board butted together at 45° is less conspicuous than a square, 90° cut. If you need to patch in a piece of new skirting, tap some wedges in behind the board to ease it away from the wall slightly and create room for the saw blade. Guide the saw with a mitre block to make a 45° cut, and then use the piece you remove as a pattern when you cut the replacement to length.

Preparing to clad a wall with tongue-and-groove panelling

Tongue-and-groove panelling is both attractive and hardwearing. It can cover an entire wall but is often only used up to the height of the dado rail.

Buying and preparing boards

Work out how many boards you need by measuring the height and width of the area you want to cover but remember that

Cover width

because the boards interlock, the width of a board is greater than the width it will cover. Allow for separate pieces of board above door frames and above and below windows. If the wall height is considerably more than the board length, fit the boards in staggered long and short upper and lower panels. Or fix the boards horizontally.

Buy all the boards at the same time and check that they are of a similar appearance – characteristics such as knots and grain pattern can vary from pack to pack. Buy boards about three weeks before you intend to put them up, and stack them flat in the room to be lined. This allows the moisture content to even out and lessens the risk of joints being pulled apart by boards shrinking.

Fixing battens to a wall

Use sawn timber battens 40mm wide and 20mm thick, treated with wood preservative. Fix them to the wall with hammer-in fixings or countersunk screws and wall plugs. For vertical boarding, fix the battens horizontally. For horizontal boarding, fix the battens vertically. The skirting board can be left in place unless you want to remove it.

ALLOWING FOR VENTILATION

In kitchens and bathrooms, where condensation is likely, allow for airflow behind the panelling.

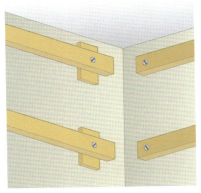

Pack behind horizontal battens with hardboard or thin plywood to lift them away from the wall. Also leave a gap at the top and bottom of the cladding. With vertical battens there is an automatic airflow if a 3mm gap is left at the top and bottom of the panelling. Use only vertical panelling on horizontal battens in kitchens and bathrooms because water can collect in the channelling of horizontal boards.

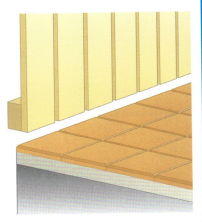

Stop the panelling slightly clear of a kitchen work surface, to prevent it getting wet, and 25mm or more clear of the top of a bath.

• Place battens at intervals of 400–500mm for 9mm thick boards, or at 500–600mm intervals for 12mm thick boards.

• The fixing should be long enough to penetrate at least 25mm into the wall.

• To ensure a level surface for the panelling, find the highest point of the wall, and mark a guideline on the floor or skirting board for the batten surface.

• To fit vertical battens, measure and draw lines down the wall at the required spacing. The battens will be fixed centrally on these lines. Before driving the fixings fully home, use a plumb line to check that each batten is vertical. Pack behind the batten where necessary. Fix battens around all window and door openings and any fixtures in the room, and ensure they align horizontally and vertically with other battens.

• When fitting battens horizontally, use a spirit level to ensure that each is horizontal.

• Check that the batten surfaces are all level with each other using either a spirit level or a plumb line dropped to the marked guideline. Pack behind battens with hardboard pieces where necessary to maintain a level surface.

HOW BOARDS FIT TOGETHER

Boards for wood panelling are long and narrow, and are mostly jointed together on their long edges. Solid timber panelling is usually varnished to keep it clean and prevent it from darkening.

Tongued-and-grooved with narrow V

The commonest type; generally 95–100mm wide, with a cover width of about 90mm. When the tongue is fitted into the groove of the adjoining board a narrow V-shaped channel is visible between boards.

Tongued-and-grooved with wide V

The channel formed between the boards is slightly wider than for the narrow V type, but the size and cover width of the board is generally the same.

Tongued-and-grooved with double V

The board has a wide V-joint and an extra groove cut down its centre to give the appearance of narrower panelling. The board is wider than other tongued-and-grooved types – generally 120mm with a cover width of 110mm.

Shiplap Each board has an L-shaped edge and a curved edge. The boards fit together with the overlap over the curve, forming a channel curved along one side. When fitting boards horizontally, place the curved edge at the top. Boards may be wider than average: 120mm with a 110mm cover width.

Square-edged Square-edged boards can be overlapped louvre fashion or they can be spaced with narrow channels that reveal the wall behind. Thick boards are normally used and they can be fitted without using a batten framework.

Lining a wall with tongue-and-groove panelling

Do not fit boards right up to wall edges. Leave a small gap of about 3mm to allow for board expansion. If ventilation is not required, any gaps can be covered with a strip of moulding.

Stop panelling several centimetres short of a fireplace or a boiler, if you can, and use tiles or plasterboard as a surround. If you cannot stop the panelling short, protect the board edges with a metal edging strip. When fitting panelling to the wall horizontally, start at the bottom.

Tools *Spirit level; steel straightedge; steel tape measure; hammer; tongued-and-grooved board off-cut; mallet. Possibly also power saw; screwdriver; nail punch; plane; gauge made from a batten marked with the width of two or three fitted boards; try-square; push-pin magnetic nail holder.*

Materials *Tongued-and-grooved boards; nails, clips, screws or panel adhesive. Possibly moulding; wood filler.*

Before you start Leave electrical fittings in position if possible and line round them so that they are recessed within the panelling.
Decide which of the following methods you will use to fix the boards:

HELPFUL TIPS

- When secret nailing thin dry boards such as pine, drill a pilot hole right through the board to avoid splitting the tongue.
- If a board is difficult to slot in straight, hammer it lightly with a mallet, using a board offcut between the board and the mallet. Slot the offcut groove over the tongue of the board that you are fitting.
- Avoid fitting boards together too tightly in kitchens and bathrooms, because humidity will cause the wood to swell and expand.

Face-nailing Use 30mm thin lost-head or oval nails or panel pins. Position them at least 15mm in from the board edge. Drive them straight in, using a nail punch. Leave the head either flush with the surface or just below it. Nails with the head left exposed should be arranged in a uniform pattern. Where nails are punched just below the surface, fill the holes with wood filler.

Screwing Usually used only for fixing square edged boards, but advisable where a tongue-and-groove board may have to be removed to get at a covered-in fitting. Use 30mm roundhead or countersunk screws. Drill holes through boards before screwing.

Secret nailing A method of nailing so that nails holding the panelling cannot be seen. Use 30mm thin lost-head or oval nails or panel pins. Hammer the nails in at an angle through the tongue of the board. Use a thin nail punch when the head gets near to the board, and drive the nail in until the corner of the head just protrudes. If the nail is driven in too far, the tongue is likely to split. The nail head is hidden when the groove of the next board is fitted over the tongue.

Nail vertical boards with the tongue on the right if you are right handed, on the left if left-handed. Nail horizontal boards with the tongue upwards. Some face-nailing is needed for boards fitted at the edge of the panelling.

Fixing boards to battens

1 Position the first board at right angles to the wall battens and about 3mm from the edge of the adjoining wall. Fit the grooved edge of a tongued-and-grooved board to the wall.

2 Use a spirit level to check that the board is vertical or horizontal.

3 Fix the board to the battens using the chosen method (left).

4 Fix the second board, using a straight-edge to check the ends are aligned with the first board, and a spirit level to make sure that it is level.

5 Continue fitting boards in the same way. The last board may have to be trimmed to fit the remaining space. When trimming, allow for a 3mm gap against the wall. If using secret nailing, secure the last board either with panel adhesive or by face nailing.

Fitting boards round doors and windows

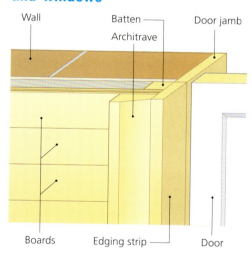

Wall — Batten — Architrave — Door jamb — Boards — Edging strip — Door

At doors and windows, remove any architraves (page 99). Fit vertical battens alongside a door jamb, leaving enough room for an edging strip to cover the batten and the edge of the end board.
• If desired, the edging strip can project in front of cladding and give an edge to which the architrave can be refitted.
• Line a deep window recess with cladding boards, with the external corners joined in one of the methods described below.
• Windowsill boards are difficult to remove. If the edges of a sill project, it is best to cut the cladding to shape to fit round them.

Joining boards at corners

How you join boards at corners will depend on whether the corner is internal or external (at a chimney breast, for example).

Internal corners

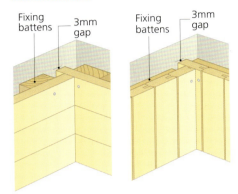

For horizontal boarding, fit one line of cladding into the corner, leaving a gap of about 3mm at the wall. Butt the panelling on the adjoining wall against it. Joints can be covered with quadrant moulding if desired.

Vertical boarding is fitted into the corner in the same way as horizontal, with the panelling butted.

External corners

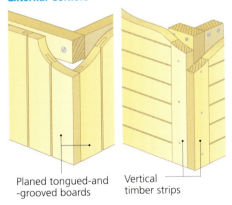

Planed tongued-and -grooved boards

Vertical timber strips

Vertical boards can be planed to remove the tongue and groove and then butted at right angles. Alternatively, you can butt the grooved edges of two boards and cover the joint with right-angled corner moulding.

For horizontal boards, fit vertical timber strips at the corner and butt the panelling boards against them.

Curing loose and squeaking boards

A floorboard squeaks because it is not firmly held to its joist. When someone steps on it, it springs under the weight, rubbing against a neighbouring board.

Not all loose boards squeak but even so they should be properly secured before a floor covering is laid, otherwise you will feel (and hear) the movement.

Replacing loose nails

A board becomes loose when one or more of its fixing nails loses its grip due to vibration or the movement of the joist below. Prise out the nail if it is still there and refix the board with a screw big enough to fill the hole left by the nail but thicker, so they bite into the joist but don't go any deeper. You don't want to puncture a hidden pipe or cable. A 50mm No. 8 screw should be suitable. The screw will hold the board securely in place, and as it goes exactly into the same hole as the nail there should be no danger of striking a cable or pipe.

Punching nails in deeper

A squeaky board can sometimes be cured by driving the nails a little deeper with a nail punch (below). Locate the punch carefully so it doesn't skid off the nail and scar the board when you strike it.

Talcum powder or chalk dust, brushed into the joints between squeaky boards, usually silences them temporarily.

Wedging with a loose board

If you can get at the underside of a squeaky board from below – to the ground floor from a cellar, for example – tap a thin wooden shim dipped in woodworking adhesive into the gap between the board and the joist.

Restoring a wood floor

An attractive floor can be created by restoring existing floorboards. Floorboards may be stripped and varnished, or you could stain, paint or lime them before sealing with a hardwearing clear coating.

Filling holes in floorboards

Use a flexible filler to cover all nail and screw heads – nail heads should be punched below the surface, and screws may need countersinking so that their heads are below the surface. If you are painting the floor, the filler colour does not matter; if you are varnishing it, choose a filler slightly lighter in colour than the surrounding floor. Once dry, sand filler flush with the floor.

RE-LAYING FLOORBOARDS

If you decide to re-lay floorboards, you need to fit the first board tight to the wall, and using a tool called a floor cramp – which can be hired – butt each board up against the previous one. Traditional cut brads are the best nails for fixing floorboards. The length of the brads should be two-and-a-half times the thickness of the boards. If you are laying a floor above an old ceiling, use screws, countersinking the heads, instead of nails so as not to risk cracking the ceiling beneath as you hammer.

Plugging gaps between boards

There are two ways to deal with gaps between floorboards: you can fill the gaps, or you can lift and relay the entire floor.

Fill narrow gaps with flexible mastic (clear mastic will be almost invisible); wider gaps are best filled with thin lengths of square-edge moulding.

Filling gaps with moulding

1 Plane moulding strips into a slight wedge shape.

2 Apply a little woodworking adhesive before tapping a wedge into a gap, thin edge first.

3 Plane wedges down to floor level when the adhesive has set, then stain them to match the boards.

Filling small gaps

Fill gaps between floorboards with a flexible acrylic flooring filler applied with a sealant gun. If you intend to sand and varnish the boards, use a ready-mixed tub filler that can be stained to match the board colour.

Restoring a woodblock floor

A woodblock (parquet or wood mosaic) floor that is not too badly damaged can be rejuvenated by sanding and sealing. The job is worth while, as such flooring is expensive and rarely fitted today. The floor may only need sanding and finishing, or you may need to replace one or more blocks.

Tools *Dust mask; nail punch and claw hammer; floor sanding machine and edging sander (a weekend's hire should be sufficient for one room); earmuffs; sanding belts (coarse, medium and fine); edging sander; old chisel; old paintbrush (for adhesive).*

Materials *Flooring varnish or other sealer; latex flooring adhesive.*

Before you start If blocks are missing, a local wood yard may be able to make replacements, or you may find them in a reclamation yard or via the Internet (try typing 'old parquet flooring' into the search engine on your computer).

1 Remove any loose blocks and scrape off the adhesive – probably black pitch – with an old chisel.

2 Spread a layer of latex adhesive into the space in the floor, about 5mm thick, using a filler knife or spatula.

3 Spread a thin layer of adhesive on the back of the block with a paintbrush and immediately put the block in place. Weigh it down by covering with a piece of plastic, a sheet of ply and several bricks, until the adhesive sets.

4 Fill any small gaps with wood filler.

5 Then use the floor sander, following directions given for sanding and varnishing a wooden floor (right). Because the grain lies in two directions, the floor must be sanded twice, running the second pass of the machine at right angles to the first.

6 The final sanding, with a very fine belt, will also need to be done in two directions to remove scratch marks.

7 Once the floor is clean and free of dust, apply your chosen finish.

Sanding and varnishing a wood floor

If floorboards are sound they can be sanded to reveal a beautiful natural floor.

Sanding a floor is hard, dusty, noisy work. On fairly new boards that have not been stained or become too dirty, sanding may not be necessary. Get rid of surface dirt by scrubbing with detergent and hot water. Pay particular attention to removing dirt from nail holes.

Tools *Dust mask; nail punch and claw hammer; floor sanding machine and edging sander (a weekend's hire should be enough for one room); earmuffs; sanding belts and discs (coarse, medium and fine); paint roller and wide paintbrush; fine steel wool.*

Materials *Flooring-grade varnish or other finish.*

Before you start Punch in all the nails in the floor, otherwise they will tear the sanding belts. Any tacks left from previous floor coverings should also be removed. If there are any traces of old polish, remove them with steel wool dipped in white spirit; otherwise the polish will clog up the sanding belt. Wear protective gloves.

WARNING

Empty the dust bag as soon as it is about one-third full. Bulked wood dust can ignite spontaneously, especially if it is impregnated with old stain or varnish. Also empty the bag whenever you stop work for more than a few minutes.

1 Start at the edge of the room with your back against the wall. Keep the sander slightly away from the skirting board at the side otherwise you may damage it.

2 It is normal to work along the length of the boards, as sanding across them causes scratches. But if the boards curl up at the edges, make the first runs diagonally across them with a coarse belt. Finish with medium and fine belts along the length of the boards.

3 On a floor where not very much stripping is needed, let the machine go forwards at a slow steady pace to the far end of the room, lifting up the drum as soon as you reach the skirting board.

4 If the boards are badly marked, wheel the sander backwards to your start point, lower the drum and make a second pass over the first one. Never pull the sander backwards when the drum is rotating, or the machine may pull sideways out of control and score the floor surface badly.

5 When the strip looks clean, move on to the next one, and continue to the end of the room. Raise the belt as you change direction, or it may damage the boards. You will have started each run about a metre out from the wall behind you. When you have covered the room, turn the machine round, and deal with that area.

Applying varnish

The quickest way of sealing a newly stripped floor is to use a paint roller to apply the varnish. Thin the first coat as recommended on the container to aid penetration, and apply full-strength for the second and third coats. Use a power sander fitted with fine abrasive paper to sand the surface lightly between coats, and wipe it with a damp cloth to remove dust before re-coating it.

1 Apply the varnish with criss-cross passes of the roller, then finish off by running it parallel with the boards.

2 Use a paintbrush to finish the floor edges and to cut in round obstacles such as central heating pipes.

Laying a wood mosaic floor

Full-size parquet blocks are not available for DIY laying, but wood mosaic, sometimes known as finger parquet, is an easy way to achieve a similar effect.

Tools *Tape measure; chalk line; workbench; fine-toothed tenon saw; trimming knife; pencil; rag. Possibly also orbital sander or sanding block; abrasive paper (medium and fine grades); hammer; paintbrush.*

Materials *Wood mosaic panels; adhesive (with spreader); wood moulding or cork strip for the edges. Possibly also panel pins for wood moulding; varnish.*

Before you start Wood mosaic comes in square panels about 10mm thick. They are usually backed by felt, paper or netting, but some makes are wired and glued together. The pieces are flexible, and can compensate for slight unevenness in the sub-floor. If the sub-floor is very uneven, cover it with hardboard first. As wood absorbs moisture from the atmosphere, buy the mosaic panels at least two days before laying, and leave them unwrapped in the room where they are to be laid. This should prevent sudden expansion or contraction.

1 Set out the mosaic, unglued, to ensure the widest border of cut tiles all around the room. As with most wood floors, a border of 15mm must be left between the edge of the mosaic and the skirting board to allow for expansion. Start laying mosaic panels from the middle of the room.

2 Where possible, arrange the laying so that the panels can be cut between 'fingers' of wood, which only involves cutting the backing with a trimming knife.

3 When you have to cut through wood, hold the panel firmly on a workbench and use a tenon saw.

4 Use the manufacturer's recommended adhesive and spread a little at a time on the prepared floor. Lay the tiles in position, pressing them into place.

5 When you have laid the floor, cover the gap around the edges with wood moulding or fill it with strips of cork.

6 Seal the surface of the finished floor with three coats of polyurethane floor sealer, thinning the first coat with 10 per cent white spirit. Sand the floor lightly between each coat and wipe off any dust with a rag dampened with white spirit.

BUYING WOOD MOSAIC

If you can, check mosaics carefully before buying. Reject any with black marks on the face. This occurs if they are stacked with the felt backing of one against the face of the other, instead of face to face, and marks can be difficult to remove. Check, too, that the panels have been cut to the same size. Take one panel and hold all the others to it in turn, back to back. Rotate each panel through 90° for a further check of squareness. Inspect the surface for chips or scratches.

Prepacked panels usually have transparent wrapping, so you can see if the panels are face to face, and you should be able to see if they are all the same size.

HOW TO REPAIR A DAMAGED MOSAIC FLOOR

If a wood mosaic floor is damaged, repair it by replacing a complete square of strips. Keep any panels left over from the original laying for repairs.

1 If possible, cut around the damaged square with a trimming knife. Cut right through the felt or paper backing.

2 Lever out the damaged square, strip by strip, using an old chisel. Be careful not to damage the adjoining piece. Scrape off the old backing and adhesive from the sub-floor.

3 Cut a new square from a spare panel, together with its backing, and glue it in place.

Laying a laminate floor

A quick way to give a room a fresh, modern makeover is to lay laminate flooring. There are two main laying systems for laminate floors: locking and tongue-and-groove.

Tools *Tape measure; pencil; scissors; trimming knife; tenon saw; hand saw or jigsaw with laminate blade; hammer; tapping block or board offcut; pulling bar; power drill with flat wood bit.*

Materials *Enough underlay and laminate flooring to cover the room; adhesive tape; PVA woodworking adhesive; edging; threshold strip; panel pins; expansion strip (optional); fitting kit (which includes wedges or spacers and pulling bar).*

Putting down an underlay

An underlay must be put down before laying any type of laminate floor. This cushions the new floor and absorbs slight irregularities in the sub-floor. If you are covering a solid floor, lay a damp-proof membrane before putting down underlay. You can buy a combined underlay and damp-proof membrane, which means fitting one layer instead of two.

1 Prepare timber floors by punching in any floorboard nails with a nail punch.

2 If you have a solid concrete floor, cover it with a layer of heavy-duty polythene sheeting to protect the laminate from any dampness within the floor.

3 Lay underlay over the whole floor, trimming to fit with scissors or a trimming knife and leaving a 10mm gap round pipes.

SOLID WOOD FLOORING

Solid wood flooring can be laid over a timber sub-floor, or directly onto floor joists. On a timber sub-floor, the boards are laid as for laminate flooring, with an expansion gap around the perimeter of the floor area. Each board is fixed using a secret nailing (see page 86).

1 Drive panel pins down through the tongue of each board at an angle to the floor so it passes through the body of the strip and into the sub-floor. Use 30mm pins for boards up to 20mm thick, and 50mm pins for thicker boards.

2 Start the pins with the hammer. Use a nail punch to finish driving each pin so its head finishes flush with the top edge of the tongue. You can then slot the grooved edge of the next board over the tongue and repeat the fixing to secure it to the sub-floor.

4 Butt joins together – do not overlap them. Secure joins with tape. If using a wood fibre underlay, allow the boards to acclimatise for 24 hours in the room before laying them, and leave an expansion gap of 5mm between the boards and 10mm round the room.

Laying locking laminate

1 Start laying the first board parallel to the longest wall in the room, in a left-hand corner, putting the end with the short tongue against the wall. Insert spacers at intervals between the skirting board and the long edge and end of the board to create an expansion gap.

2 Add more boards until you reach the end of the row, where you will probably need to cut a board.

3 If the offcut is longer than 300mm, use it to start the second row. Otherwise, cut a board in half and use that. This ensures that the joints will be staggered between the rows. Fit spacers at the end.

4 Carry on placing the boards row by row. As you finish each row, enlist help to lift the row so that the long edge is at an angle of about 30° to the previous row, and lower and push down the boards to lock the rows together.

5 At the last row you will probably have to cut the final boards down in width. Lay each board in turn over the last whole board laid, and mark the width required on it by using a pencil and a board offcut held against the skirting board to scribe the wall profile on it.

6 Redraw the line 5mm nearer the exposed edge of the board to re-create the expansion gap. Cut each board to width with a jigsaw or panel saw and fit in place.

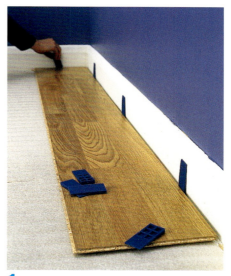

1 Lay the first board parallel to the longest wall in the room, with its groove facing the wall. Insert spacers to create a 10mm expansion gap.

2 Lay the next plank end-on to the first one, fitting the tongue into the groove.

7 Remove the spacers from the edge of the flooring and conceal the expansion gap with strips of trim to match the floor. In corners, cut the moulding at 45°, using a mitre block. Use glue or nails to fix the trim to the skirting, not to the floor.

Laying tongue-and-groove laminate

The process is largely the same as for locking laminate (left). However, because gluing does not allow for mistakes, prepare and lay two or three rows without gluing to check the fit first. Always lay boards with the tongue protruding.

3 When you have laid three whole rows, take them up and re-lay them using wood adhesive. Tap them together with the hammer and tapping block.

4 Wipe off any oozing adhesive straight away with a damp rag. Do this again once you have closed up the joints (overleaf).

5 At the end of the row, use the pulling bar to close up the joint by hooking it over the end of the board and tapping the upstand with a hammer.

6 Start the next row with the offcut from the previous row to create offset joints. Glue the grooved edge and push it into place.

7 As you work across the room, tap the boards closely together by using a proprietary tapping block and hammer to close up the joints.

8 Follow steps 5, 6 and 7 of Laying locking laminate (page 95) to fit the last row and hide the expansion gap.

Fitting boards round pipes

1 To cut round a radiator pipe, align the board with its neighbour and slide it up against the pipe.

2 Mark the pipe centre on the board edge. Then remove the board, butt it up against the skirting board and mark the pipe centre on the board's short end. Join up the marks to indicate the pipe centre.

3 Use a 16mm flat wood bit to drill a hole through the board at the mark. Cut across the board and fit the two sections round the pipe.

Alternatively Almost all laminate floors come with optional accessory kits, including radiator pipe discs. These have a hole cut for the pipe: simply align the grain and glue into place to hide ragged holes.

At door openings

Cut away a small amount of the architrave and door stop to allow the board to fit beneath it. Mark the board thickness on the frame and cut away the wood with a

tenon saw. Trim the board to shape and slot it into position. Fit a threshold bar across the door to conceal and protect the edge of the flooring. Cut the bar to the right width and glue or screw it into place.

Fixing creaking stairs

Stairs creak when a tread or riser is not securely fixed and rubs against an adjacent piece of wood. The cure is straightforward if the underside of the staircase is accessible.

Determine which tread is creaking. If you have a cupboard under the stairs, ask someone to walk slowly up the stairs: you should be able to see which treads are flexing as well as hear the creak.

Working from underneath

The best remedy is to add extra wood angle blocks, screwed and glued to the tread and riser from underneath.

Tools *Saw; bradawl; drill and twist bits; screwdriver.*

Materials *Blocks of wood about 40mm triangular or square in section and about 75mm long; PVA adhesive; four No. 8 screws per block (choose a length that will not break through the face of the stair).*

1 Drill four clearance holes in each block – one pair at right angles to the other.

2 Apply PVA adhesive to the blocks and push them in place.

3 Secure the blocks to the tread and riser with four screws.

4 If possible, strengthen the join between the riser and the tread below by squeezing PVA adhesive into the join. Then drive three evenly spaced screws horizontally through the riser and into the tread. Position the screws 12mm up from the bottom of the riser.

Working from above

You will have to lift the stair carpet to work on the treads. Try brushing some talcum powder into the squeaking join to act as a lubricant. If the squeak continues, screw down the front of the tread onto the riser.

Tools *Old chisel; drill and twist bits; countersink bit; screwdriver; filling knife; abrasive paper.*

Materials *PVA adhesive; 38mm No. 8 countersunk screws; filler.*

1 Using a chisel, force apart the top of the riser and the tread above, and insert some glue in the space: this is only possible if the treads and risers are not jointed together.

2 Drill clearance holes every 250mm through the tread and pilot holes into the top of the riser. Countersink the clearance holes so screws will sit below surface level. Insert the screws and screw down tight.

3 Cover screw heads with filler and smooth with abrasive paper. If the stairs are varnished, use a matching wood filler.

Repairing broken balusters

If you still have all the pieces, it may be possible to mend a damaged baluster. If the damage is severe, you will have to replace it.

Tools *Mallet; old chisel; handsaw; hammer; vice clamp.*

Materials *New baluster if needed; nails (same length as the old ones).*

Before you start Examine the broken baluster: if it has split or a piece has broken off, apply PVA adhesive to the two surfaces and bind them with insulating tape. Clamp the baluster between two blocks of wood until the adhesive has dried. Remove the tape and smooth with fine abrasive paper.

1 Free the baluster at the bottom. If the outer string is open (where the sides of the stairs have a zigzag profile with the treads resting on the horizontal section) prise off the cover moulding on the side of the tread. Then gently tap the bottom end of the baluster out of its slot with a mallet.

If the outer string is 'closed' (its top and bottom edges are parallel and the tread and riser slot into grooves), a baluster on an old staircase may be held in a mortise or it may be pinned. Scrape away the paint to check. If it is mortised use a handsaw to cut through it at the bottom following the line of the string. If it is pinned, knock it out with the mallet.

Alternatively On a modern staircase it may be held at the bottom between fillets of wood. Lift out the broken baluster, and lever out the lower fillet.

2 Remove the top part of the broken baluster by tapping it with a mallet so it is freed from the rail. If there is no space between the balusters to wield the mallet, place the end of a piece of wood against the baluster and tap the other end with the mallet. Or pull out the baluster by hand.

3 Use the broken baluster as a pattern to mark the correct slope on the top of the new one. Before you cut it to length, make sure that you have got the measurement right.

4 Hold the new baluster in a vice and cut along the marked line.

5 On an open (cut) string, fit it back in place in its notch on the tread and nail the baluster to the handrail at the top.
  On a closed string, use the old baluster to cut the angle at the bottom and fit the new one in place, top and bottom. If the baluster was originally mortised into the string, it will have to be nailed in place. The repair will not be as strong as the original.
  If you have to replace a fillet, tack it in place. A nail punch will help you to work in an awkward space.

Finding a match

Replacement balusters can be hard to find, but look around local architectural salvage yards before paying a wood turner to reproduce just one or two.

FIXING LOOSE BALUSTERS

Balusters are usually fixed to the handrail by nails driven through them at an angle, and into the underside of the rail. Sometimes they are fitted between fillets of wood.

Nailing the baluster If a nail works loose, try to remove it with pincers, and insert a longer, slightly thicker nail in its place. If you can't remove it, drive another one in at a different place. On slender balusters drill a fine pilot hole first. Do not use glue. The baluster may have to be removed at some time in the future.

Replacing a fillet The balusters must be fitted into a groove in the underside of the rail, with the spaces between balusters filled with fillets of wood. If a fillet has dropped out, cut a new piece of wood to the right size and nail it in place. Do not use glue. A nail punch will help to drive the nail in. Baluster fillets can be bought at some DIY stores, but they may not fit your staircase.

Putting up or replacing architraves

Architraves are strips of timber moulding used to cover a joint between woodwork and a wall, such as round a door or window frame. They can be decorative or plain.

Tools *Trimming knife; chisel; pencil; mitre saw or mitre box and tenon saw; hammer; nail punch; cartridge gun.*

Materials *Architrave moulding; scrap wood; 38mm oval wire nails; woodworking adhesive; 25mm panel pins; acrylic mastic.*

Before you start Ensure new mouldings are straight, flat and as wide as any you are replacing. If they are narrower, you will need to redecorate the wall round the door, and there will be a gap between the architrave and the skirting board. If the mouldings are wider, notch the ends of the side pieces so they fit round skirting boards.

1 If you are removing an old architrave, run a knife blade between the architrave and the door frame to break the paint seal. Prise off the top section with a wide chisel while using scrap wood to protect the wall.

2 Remove the two side mouldings. Insert the blade of the chisel under a moulding from the wall edge if you can; otherwise, slide it between moulding and door frame.

3 Position a length of new moulding against the door frame, with the bottom edge of the moulding resting on the floor. Mark the position of the inside of the mitre joint on it with a pencil. Check you are sawing in the right direction, then cut the mitre, using a mitre box and tenon saw, or a precision mitre saw.

4 Hold the moulding against the door frame, line up its inner edge with the paint line on the frame and hammer nails into the moulding. Space the nails about 450mm apart. Use a nail punch to drive the heads just below the surface. Fit the other side moulding in the same way.

5 Before fixing the top section in place, place a short length of moulding upside down across the tops of the side mouldings, and mark on it the positions of the mitre joints. Then cut the two mitres at the marks and sand the edges smooth.

6 Add a little woodworking adhesive to each end of the top section, then position the section between the side mouldings. Fix it to the door frame with two nails. Use a damp cloth to remove any visible adhesive.

Curing faults in doors

Many faults in doors can be cured quite easily. For some jobs you may need another person to help you, or to steady the door while you work on it.

Door panels split

Sometimes splits develop in the panels of old doors. The solution depends on whether the door is painted or varnished.

Painted door
On a painted door, fill the crack with a wood filler and paint over it.

Natural wood door
On a varnished door where the filler will show, drive dowels into the edge of the door to press against the edges of the panel and close the crack.

1 First clean out old varnish or filler from the crack with a sharp knife.

2 Drill two or three 8mm diameter holes through the edge of the door to line up with the near edge of the panel. Measure the thickness of the door stile and mark the drill bit with a piece of tape to act as a depth stop.

3 Cut some 8mm dowels about 20mm longer than the width of the stiles.

4 Squirt PVA wood adhesive into the crack in the panel and into the holes in the stile. Drive the dowels into the holes so they press against the edge of the panel and close the crack.

3 There should be a slight gap between the edge of the door and the frame. To check for this, run a thin knife blade all round the edge of the door when it is closed. Where the gap is insufficient, strip and then plane that edge of the door. You may have to take the door off its hinges, and perhaps remove locks and latches.

4 Prime and paint the stripped edges of the door. Then let the paint dry before closing the door.

Door binding at bottom or top

If an external door binds at its lower corners, the problem is often caused by moisture being absorbed through an unpainted bottom edge. Take door off its hinges and dry the barewood with a hot-air gun. Apply two coats of quick-drying wood primer and re-hang when it is touch dry.

If a door is sticking at the top you may be able to plane it without taking it off its hinges by propping it open with wedges and working from a stepladder.

5 Wipe off excess adhesive with a damp cloth. Leave the protruding dowel until the glue has set, then trim it off flush with the door edge. Smooth the cut end with abrasive paper.

Door binding along one side

Doors often bind (stick) in their frames because regular repainting causes a build-up of paint on the edge of the door and on the frame.

1 Strip off the paint. Do this mechanically to avoid damaging the finish on the door faces. Use either a power sander or a Surform planer file.

2 Smooth the stripped surfaces with glasspaper and check that the door opens and closes easily.

Door frame loose

Slamming a door often leads to the frame becoming loose. Make new fixings with three frame plugs at each side of the frame. The length of the frame plugs, which come complete with hammer-in screws, should be the thickness of the frame plus at least 60mm.

1 Using a masonry bit, drill through the frame and into the wall behind it to the required depth.

2 Hammer the screw and plug into the hole until the screw head is flush with the frame.

Door sags

When the bottom corner of the door rubs on the floor, the cause is either faulty hinges or loose joints in the door. Partly open the door and lift the handle to see if there is movement at the hinges or joints.

Faulty hinges

If the hinge screws are loose, try tightening them. If they will not hold, remove them, drill out the screw holes and plug them with glued dowels. Drill new pilot holes and refit the screws.

If the movement is in the knuckle of the hinge due to a worn hinge pin, the only cure is to fit new hinges. The hinges may not be large enough to support the weight of the door. In this case fit larger, stronger hinges, and add a third hinge midway between them if you are working on a front door.

Loose door joints

If the problem is that corner joints on a framed door are loose, glue and cramp them back into place.

1 Take the door off its hinges, and try to prise the loose joints apart.

2 Squirt woodworking adhesive into the joints and cramp them closed with sash cramps. Be sure to check that the door frame is square.

3 On the edge of the door, drive small wooden wedges into the ends of the tenons in order to prevent the joints from opening up again.

4 Drill through the face of the door and the tenon, and drive a glued dowel into the hole to lock the tenon in place.

5 Trim off the dowels flush with the surface of the door.

How to hang a front or back door

When buying a new door, measure the height and width of the frame and get a door that is either the right size or slightly too big. Get someone to help you fit it if you can.

Panelled doors can have up to 20mm removed all round to fit, but most flush doors should have no more than about 10mm planed away, otherwise they may be seriously weakened.

Flush doors contain wooden blocks for fitting hinges and locks; their positions are marked on the edges of the door. When fitting the hinges and locks, note where the blocks are, as they will affect the way round that the door is placed in the frame. If you want to reverse the face of the door, most are reversible top to bottom.

You will need three butt hinges – either 75 or 100mm long. The job will be simpler if you choose a size to fit the existing hinge recesses on the frame.

If a flush door is being fitted, buy pressed-steel cranked butt hinges (above right). A panelled door, which is heavier, requires cast butt hinges.

Tools *Pencil; tape measure; try square; marking gauge; 19mm or 25mm chisel; mallet; plane; panel or tenon saw; trimming knife; drill and twist bits; screwdriver; folding workbench.*

Materials *Exterior door; three hinges; screws to fit (check that the heads fit fully into the countersunk holes on the hinge).*

REMOVING STUBBORN SCREWS

When you remove your old door, the hinge screws may be difficult to get out. Scrape off any paint, particularly out of the slots. If a screw still will not shift, put a screwdriver in the slot and hit it with a mallet.

Removing the old door

1 Remove the old door carefully, without damaging the hinge recesses on the frame. Put pieces of wood under the door to take the weight while you remove the screws, and get someone to hold it.

2 New panelled doors are sometimes protected with strips of timber or cork pads at the edges; remove these by prising them off with a broad scraper blade.

Getting the fit right

1 Hold the door against the frame to mark it for trimming. A glass-panelled door is usually fitted with the putty on the outside and decorative wood beading on the inside.

2 When the door is centrally positioned, get someone to steady it, and put wedges underneath to hold it at the correct height.

3 Lightly mark the face with a soft pencil to give the correct gap round the perimeter. A panelled door should have a gap of 3mm all round to allow the wood to swell in wet weather. A flush door should have a gap of 2mm. If the frame is straight you may not have to trim all the edges of the door. However, if the frame is out of true, or if there is a fair amount of trimming to do, it will be necessary to trim all round.

4 If there is more than about 5mm of wood to remove, lay the door flat on boxes or trestles and saw it close to the trimming line, then finish off with a plane.

5 For planing, hold the door on its edge in the jaws of a folding adjustable workbench. Protect the bottom edge on scrap timber and then plane the top edge down to the pencilled trimming line.

6 Plane the long edges of the door in the direction of the grain. The shavings will be removed smoothly, whereas if you plane against the grain the blade will tend to dig into the wood.

7 Plane the top and bottom edges of the door from each side towards the centre. This will avoid splitting wood at the edge of the stiles where you will be planing across the grain.

8 Stand the door in the frame on wedges and check there is the right gap all round.

9 When the fit is correct, plane a slight slope on the edges of both door stiles towards the doorstop on the frame. This will ensure that the door will close easily without binding against the frame.

Hanging the door

1 Hold the door in the frame to mark the hinge positions. If the hinge recesses in the frame are already cut to the right size, mark the top and bottom of the recesses on the edge of the door. If not, increase the size with a chisel as explained below, and then mark the top and bottom of the hinge positions on the door.

2 Hold the hinge in place on the door and mark round the edge of each hinge flap with a trimming knife. With a cranked butt hinge the whole knuckle of the hinge should project from the face of the door and from the frame. With a cast butt hinge the centre of the knuckle should be in line with the face of the door and frame.

3 Mark the thickness of the flap on the door face with a marking gauge.

4 Cut around the perimeter of the hinge recess with a sharp chisel. Then make a series of cuts about 5mm apart across the grain of the wood, and carefully pare away the waste.

5 Screw the hinge flaps into the recesses in the door, putting only one screw in each hinge for the time being.

6 Hold the door open on wedges and screw the hinges to the frame – again using one screw each. Each screw head should lie flush with the surface of the hinge flap.

If the screw heads protrude, they will bind and prevent the door from closing. You can either deepen the countersinks in the hinge with a high-speed-steel twist bit in a power drill, or else you could buy screws one gauge size smaller.

If the screws do not tighten into the frame, glue pieces of dowel in the old screw holes and drill new ones.

7 Check that the door swings open and shut easily. If it does not close properly, the hinge positions may have to be adjusted.

8 When the door moves correctly, insert the remaining hinge screws.

Fitting a letterplate and knocker

It is a simple job to add a letterplate or a knocker to your front door. Double-check all your measurements before making the first cut in the door.

Before you start A power jigsaw makes the job of cutting the letterplate opening much quicker than doing it with a padsaw.

Letterplate

There are many different designs available for letterplates. Some incorporate a handle which can be used as a door-knocker.

Tools *Pencil; ruler; power drill and twist bits; 13mm flat wood bit; jigsaw or padsaw; chisel; abrasive paper; screwdriver; small adjustable spanner; hacksaw.*

Materials *Letterplate and fittings.*

1 Decide where you want the letterplate. On a panel door it can be fitted horizontally in the middle rail or vertically on the lock stile. On a flush door, fit it horizontally in the middle to coincide with the rail position that is marked on the edge of the door.

2 Measure the size of the flap and spring mechanism and lightly mark the outline of the required cut-out with a pencil.

3 Using the flat bit, drill a 13mm hole at each corner of the cut-out position and saw along the cut-out line. Preferably use a jigsaw with a long blade. Alternatively, you can make the cut-out with a padsaw, but it will be very slow work.

4 At each side of the cut-out, mark the positions of the holes for the fixing bolts.

5 Working from the front of the door, drill 13mm diameter holes to a depth of 13mm to accommodate the fixing lugs of the letterplate.

6 Using a twist bit the same diameter as the fixing bolts, drill from the centre of the holes right through the door.
   Smooth the edges of the holes with abrasive paper.

7 Fit the letterplate to the door and then tighten the fixing nuts with an adjustable spanner.

8 If the bolts protrude, use a hacksaw to cut them off flush with the face of the nuts.

Door knocker

1 Hold the knocker in position and press it hard against the door so that the lugs leave light marks.

2 At these positions, drill holes for the lugs and the bolts.

3 Screw the bolts into the lugs on the back of the knocker, and push them through the holes.

4 Tighten the fixing nuts, and if the bolts protrude cut them off flush with the face of the nuts.

Replacing broken sash cords

When a sash cord breaks, replace all four cords on the window. The other three are probably failing, too.

Tools *Old chisel; string; trimming knife; pincers; screwdriver; hammer; small weight (a screw will do); matches. Perhaps machine oil.*

Materials *Sash cords (preferably Terylene); 25mm galvanised clout (large head) nails; 25mm oval nails; filler.*

Taking out the sashes

1 Working from inside the room, prise off the staff beads from the front of the window frame on each side. An old chisel or a large screwdriver is a suitable tool for the job.

Start at the centre of the staff bead to avoid damaging the mitre joints at the top and bottom. Once they have been lifted at the centre, the staff beads can be sprung out of place.

2 Lift the bottom sash out of the window as far as it will go. Rest it on a table or a portable workbench or ask someone to hold it for you.

3 Tie the end of a ball of string to the upper part of each cord (if the cords are not already broken).

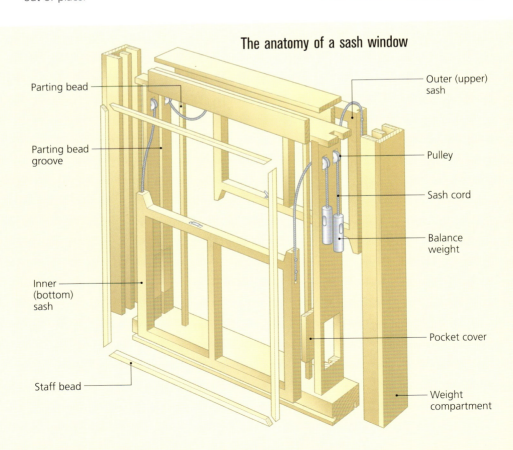

The anatomy of a sash window

Parting bead

Parting bead groove

Inner (bottom) sash

Staff bead

Outer (upper) sash

Pulley

Sash cord

Balance weight

Pocket cover

Weight compartment

4 Hold each cord in turn, and cut through it with a trimming knife. Release it gently to lower the balance weight to the bottom of the box. This will draw the string over the pulley. The string will be used to thread the new cord. Set the released sash to one side.

5 Prise the narrow parting beads out of their grooves. If they have been nailed (incorrectly) rather than merely wedged in place, remove the nails with pincers, taking care not to split the beads.

If they are already split, buy new beads and cut them to length.

6 Lift the top sash into the room. If the cords are unbroken, tie string to the upper part and then cut the cords in the same way as before.

Fixing the cords to the weights

1 When measuring up for new cords, measure from the top of the window down to the sill, and add two-thirds again. This will allow enough spare cord for fixing at each end. Cut four pieces of cord to this length – one for each weight.

2 With the chisel, carefully prise the pocket covers from the weight channel at each side of the frame, towards the bottom. Usually they are just pushed in place, but sometimes they are screwed.

3 Reach into the pockets and lift the weights (two on each side) into the room. Leave the strings in place over the pulleys, ready to pull the new cords through.

HELPFUL TIP

If you have no one to help you nail the cord to the side of the sash, pull the weight up to the top of its compartment and wind the cord around a screwdriver. It will hold the weight while you nail the other end of the cord in place.

Alternatively Jam a wedge, such as a pencil, between the cord and the top of the pulley aperture.

4 Where cords have broken, tie a 'mouse' (any small weight – a screw will do) to a length of string and push it over the pulley, so that it drops down into the weight compartment and can be drawn out through the pocket.

5 Use a screwdriver to push the old pieces of cord out of the sash weights.

6 Remove the old cords from the grooves in the side of the window sashes. They are held with clout (large-head) nails which can be extracted with pincers.

7 Tie the end of the new cord to the string coming from one of the rear pulleys. Pull it over the pulley, into the weight compartment, and out through the pocket.

8 Untie the string, and tie the new cord to the balance weight, using a double knot. To prevent Terylene cord from fraying, heat the end with a match to melt the fibres into a solid lump.

9 Replace the weight in the pocket. Repeat the process for all four weights, then fit the pocket covers in place; they should not be nailed or glued.

Fixing the cords to the sashes

1 Rest the top (outer) sash on the inside window ledge.

2 Get a helper to pull down one of the cords so that the weight is at the top of its compartment and just touching the pulley.

3 Screw or nail the cord into the groove at the side of the sash, using galvanised screws or clout (large-head) nails. Do not fit the screws or nails close to the top of the groove; they will prevent the sash sliding all the way up. The top screw or nail must be no higher than the distance from the mid-point of the pulley to the top of the frame.

4 Repeat for the second cord.

5 Put the sash in place and check that it operates smoothly before you reassemble the window.

Reassembling the window

1 Refit the parting beads between the runners on each side, tapping them into the grooves so they will not move.

2 Attach the sash cords to the lower (inner) sash in the same way as the upper sash. Then fit the sash in position in the frame.

3 Refit the staff beads on each side of the frame, checking that the mitred ends match up neatly with the beads at the top and bottom. Fix them without glue, using two or three oval nails so that they will be easy to remove in the future. Do not drive the nails fully home yet.

4 Check that the lower sash operates easily. If it rattles in its runners move the beads slightly closer to the sash. If not, drive the nails home. If the staff beads are damaged, replace them with lengths of new beading mitred at each end.

5 Repair any damaged areas around the frame with wood filler. When it is dry, smooth with abrasive paper and touch up the repairs with paint.

Renewing parting beads and staff beads

Before you can renew the beads, remove the damaged ones as described under Replacing broken sash cords (page 106).

Renewing parting beads

1 Buy new parting beads the same dimensions as the old ones or slightly larger and plane them down. Cut the beads to the height of the inner frame.

2 With a plane, take a few shavings off the length of the bead on each side, towards the edge that will fit into the groove. This slight taper will ensure that the bead is a tight fit.

3 Tap the beads into the grooves; there is no need to nail them.

Renewing staff beads

Buy new staff beads the same dimensions as the old ones. Alternatively, buy new ones as close as possible in shape, and long enough to go all round the frame. You will need slightly more than the measurement of the frame to allow a little wastage for mitres to be cut at each corner.

1 Cut a 45° mitre at one end of a length of bead, using a mitre box to ensure an accurate cut.

2 Hold the bead against the frame with the mitre pressed into a corner and mark with a pencil where the other mitre is to be cut.

3 Cut a second mitre, and repeat for each length of beading all round the frame.

4 When all the lengths have been cut, wedge them in place and examine the corner joints for fit.

5 Fix each bead in place with two or three 25mm oval nails.

Furniture
restoration

Blemishes

Wooden furniture is easily scratched, knocked or stained but in most cases simple repairs can be made to rectify the damage.

Checking the finish

Before you can repair the damage to wooden furniture you must first identify the finish. Wax, lacquer, French polish and different varnishes all require different treatment.

How to tell wax from oil

Try the white spirit test to distinguish between a waxed and an oiled surface. Dampen a cloth with a little of the solvent and wipe a hidden corner of the item of furniture. If the surface finish dissolves and leaves a smear on the cloth, it has been waxed; if it turns slippery but does not smear, an oil finish has been applied to it.

Spotting varnishes and lacquers

Check the surface for discoloration. Cellulose lacquer and acrylic varnish are almost completely clear when dry, while polyurethane varnish yellows with time. You could also rub a little cellulose thinners on a hidden spot. A lacquered or acrylic varnish finish will rapidly dissolve; one coated with polyurethane varnish will be unaffected. Alternatively, try scraping a hidden area with a trimming knife (below). Polyurethane varnish lifts in flakes and dust, a cold-cure lacquer as dust only.

Identifying French polish

Find out if a piece of furniture is finished with French polish by rubbing an inconspicuous area with a cloth dipped in methylated spirits. If it is, the surface will soften in seconds and leave smears on the cloth.

Fast face-lifts and disguises

Scorch marks

Most burns in wooden furniture are caused by cigarettes or cigars. There is no quick fix or chemical cure for a burn; the black mark must be scraped out with a trimming knife or chisel. You'll then need to fill and camouflage the resulting depression. Depending on the depth of the gouge and the finish of the surface you are repairing, use either a wax stick or matching wood stopping.

Heat makes French polish craze. Restore the finish by flicking some baby oil onto the surface, then rub it over gently with a cloth dampened in methylated spirits.

Ink blots

You can use oxalic acid to bleach ink stains out of furniture, but a much safer alternative for bare wood is to rub salt and lemon juice over the stain. On a finished surface, ink blots are best ignored, especially if the piece of furniture is an old desk or bureau.

Scratches

A felt-tip pen that matches the colour of the finish is good for camouflaging scratches (above), but if you want to fill the blemish, thicken up the right shade of artist's oil paint with clear furniture wax and apply it with an artist's brush. A patch of scratches can often be disguised by gently rubbing the area with fine garnet paper, moistened with linseed oil, and then polishing it.

In varnish Use clear nail polish as a filler for chips and scratches in varnish. Overfill the damage and leave the nail polish to harden thoroughly before carefully rubbing it down with a fine grade wet-and-dry abrasive paper.

In polyurethane varnish Use Danish oil to disguise scratches on polyurethane varnished surfaces. Once the oil has dried – after about 4 hours – wipe the surface with clear wax.

In French polish You can disguise superficial scratches on French-polished surfaces with a concoction used by antique restorers. Pour equal volumes of white spirit, methylated spirits and linseed oil into a container, then shake the mixture thoroughly before using it. Use a clean soft cloth to apply it to the scratched area, rubbing with a circular motion.

White ring stains

If the white ring mark penetrates to the wood, you will have to strip and refinish the wood. However, if the mark has affected only the finish of the wood, you may be able to remove it yourself.

On French polish Try rubbing the white ring vigorously with a cloth dipped in metal polish or car rubbing compound. Both are abrasive so apply them gently with a soft damp cloth.

On wax Make a paste out of salt and olive oil. Spread it over the ring and leave it overnight. Next day, wipe it off and rewax the affected area.

Dust and grime

Clean away layers of dust-ingrained wax with a homemade furniture cleaner, made up of equal quantities of vinegar, white spirit and water. Add a squirt of washing-up liquid to the mixture, then apply with a house-plant spray. Wipe off the liquefied residue before it hardens.

SAFETY PRECAUTION

Many of the materials used to refinish furniture are flammable and give off noxious fumes. Work in well-ventilated spaces and don't smoke.

Repairs

You can make easy repairs to cracks in wooden furniture using wax or wood fillers. You may have to take the furniture apart to make some repairs.

Holes, cracks and gouges

Dents and cracks are common problems on wooden furniture but on most solid surfaces they can be easily repaired with wood filler. Not all holes are caused by wear and tear however. Woodworm lay their eggs in wood and cause a huge amount of damage.

Detecting and dealing with woodworm

Check for active woodworm by looking out for tiny tell-tale piles of sawdust at the bottom of cupboards and drawers, and particularly around the parts of a piece of furniture that haven't been painted or varnished: the beetle prefers to eat its way out through bare wood.

Dark woodworm holes are the sign of an old infestation, but treat the piece of furniture with woodworm killer anyway: if there are larvae in the wood, they will be killed, while adult beetles won't lay eggs in treated wood. Paint all surfaces of furniture with two coats of woodworm killer and inject some exit holes with a proprietary woodworm killer with a special nozzle (see above).

Wear safety spectacles or goggles when injecting fluid into exit holes; it can shoot out of other holes into your eyes.

Disguising woodworm damage

Disguise woodworm holes with wax or a wood filler. As well as making the damage less conspicuous, a fresh attack will be easier to spot.

You can use glass-fibre resin, available from car accessory shops, to reinforce furniture that has been badly weakened by woodworm. Drill small holes about 6mm ($1/4$in) or less in diameter around the damaged area and force the resin into them. It will set solid. Damaged cupboard hinge areas on chipboard units can be reinforced in the same way.

Filling cracks and holes

Wax filler stick Use a matching wax filler stick to fill fine cracks. Remove any surplus with fine abrasive paper which has been moistened with linseed oil.

Wood filler For large cracks, fill the crack slightly proud of the surface with a matching wood filler. When it has set, sand it smooth, working with the grain of the wood. If there is a strain on the wood that may cause a crack to open again, use a two-part epoxy wood filler, which is much stronger.

Children's wax crayons These make a fast-setting stopper if you cannot get hold of any wax filling sticks. Melt the crayon in a spoon over a candle, blending hot wax from different coloured crayons to match the piece of furniture. Trickle the molten wax into small gouges, deep scratches and woodworm holes, smoothing it with a knife dipped in hot water. Use a plastic scraper to remove the excess wax once it hardens.

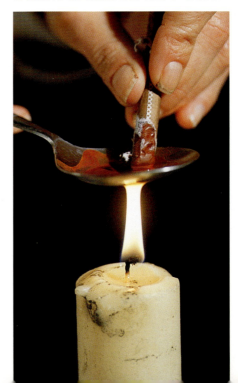

Shellac filler Shellac sticks are sold for repairing damage and stopping up holes in furniture finished with French polish. You can also use liquid shellac (normal French polish). Pour it into a saucer and leave it for 30 minutes or so to thicken. Pick up some of the viscous shellac on the end of a matchstick and trickle it into the damage. Build up the repair layer by layer if necessary, then carefully scrape off the excess with a sharp blade before rubbing down with fine-grade wet-and-dry abrasive paper.

Car body filler This is an economical material for repairing damaged furniture. You can use it with solid wood and manufactured materials such as chipboard and MDF. Small screws driven into the damaged area first will help to bond the filler and to prevent it cracking away.

You can make a mould to contain the filler (and minimise the amount which has to be sanded off) with small blocks of wood tacked into place around the repair (below). Line the blocks with a clear cellulose tape such as Sellotape to prevent the filler sticking to them. Shape the final layer of filler with a trimming knife while it is soap-hard. Then smooth the repair with fine abrasive paper once it has hardened.

Dye your own filler

Instead of building up a stock of several differently coloured wood fillers, buy a single tin of light-coloured stopper. Then stain a little of it a different colour every time you want to match a different wood. Make sure that all the stains you buy are compatible with your single tin of filler.

Hiding damage with wood patches

Plug cutters and matching drill sets enable you to drill out a flaw in a piece of furniture and replace it with a plug of wood that fits snugly into the hole. Select a piece of wood with matching grain and colour to the surface being repaired from which to cut a plug, then the repair will be virtually invisible.

If you don't have a plug cutter, make a diamond-shaped insert. Plane a slight bevel on the edges of the insert before using it as a template to mark out a recess around the damage. As the insert is tapped into the recess, the bevel will ensure a really tight, invisible fit.

Taking components apart

Reinforcing loose joints

Old synthetic glue has to be carefully pared and scraped away with a chisel. Try to avoid removing any wood with the glue or the new joint will be a loose fit and will be weak.

Try injecting glue into a loose joint before you resort to taking it apart. Drill a small hole into the joint, where it cannot be easily seen, then use a plastic syringe to force new glue into the gap. PVA or urea-formaldehyde glue is the best choice. Plug the drilled hole with a blob of Plasticine or putty until the glue has set.

Loose corner joints in inconspicuous places – at the back of a bookcase, for example – can be reinforced and kept square with small triangular braces made from plywood. Glue and screw the braces, sometimes called ply webs, into place across each corner.

Removing old glue

Knocking joints apart risks damaging the components. If the piece is old, however, it will have been assembled with scotch glue, which is soluble in methylated spirits so try swabbing joints with meths. Drill a small hole to improve access to the joint if necessary, and use a plastic syringe to flood the hole with meths.

Removing nails and dowels

If a nail or dowel has been used to reinforce a mortise-and-tenon joint in a piece of furniture, you'll have to drill it out with a twist drill before you can dismantle the joint. When removing a nail, punch the head in first, so that the drill is less likely to jump off it and damage the surface of the wood as you drill out the shank. To remove a dowel, use a drill bit that matches the diameter of the dowel you will be fitting as a replacement.

Loose 'dry' dowels in mortise-and-tenon joints can be removed by driving a screw into the end of the dowel, then gripping the head of the screw with a pair of pincers and pulling it out of its hole.

SAFETY PRECAUTION

Some woodworking glues can cause skin irritation. Wear latex gloves when using urea-formaldehyde glues, such as Cascamite, and also epoxy resin glues. If any glue does get on your skin, wipe it off immediately.

Putting pieces back together

Test the fit first
Make sure that all the pieces fit together perfectly before gluing any furniture back together. This serves as a check that you've assembled joints with the right pieces of wood in the right places. It's better to discover a problem at this stage than have to undo cramps and remake the joints.

Note where cramps are best positioned during the dry run. Then tape offcuts of wood, corrugated card or pieces of hard rubber in place, to spread the pressure of the cramp jaws and stop them biting into the wood. Don't overtighten cramps – it risks forcing the joints out of square.

Wooden table
A solid wooden table top can split if it is simply screwed to its supporting frame. Replace the screws with slotted shrinkage plates, which are designed to allow the top to expand and contract independently of the frame.

Wooden chair
If you have to re-glue the stretchers between the legs of a wooden chair, make a tourniquet to hold them while the glue sets (below). Loop a length of cord around the legs – protecting the wood with corrugated card – then put a stick or screwdriver through the loop and twist it to tighten the arrangement.

Chest of drawers
Examine the drawer fronts on an old chest of drawers. There should be an even gap at the top and bottom when they are shut, but wear on the drawer runners often means the fronts 'drop' and clash on the frame ledge below, leaving all the gap at the top.

Even things up by gluing and pinning slips of thin plywood to the ledge of the frame – two for each drawer. Set the pieces of ply back from the edge slightly so they don't show. Then, when the drawers are shut, their fronts will be supported on the ply slips and the gap will be evened out.

HELPFUL TIP
If a wood panel is split you can mend it using G-cramps. If the wood is thin, glue blocks of scrap wood onto the underside or back of the panel, at either side of the split. When the blocks are firm, squeeze glue into the split, then tighten G-cramps on the blocks to force the split closed. When the glue has set, knock the blocks off with a mallet and chisel.

For thick panels, use screws to fix the blocks, but make sure they don't penetrate the face of the panel.

Stripping

Making a good job of stripping furniture requires patience, so start with small items. Leave larger items until you've gained some experience.

Chemical strippers

The best way of taking off old paint and varnish is with a chemical stripper. Sanding surfaces removes some of the wood, which can easily spoil delicate, well-defined mouldings. With a hot-air gun or blowlamp, you run the risk of charring the surface. Most chemical strippers are applied in liquid form or as a paste.

Safety guidelines

Protect your eyes and skin Wear safety goggles and protect your hands with rubber gloves. If you splash stripper on your skin, wash it off immediately.

Make yourself comfortable Stripping a piece of furniture is a long job. Make yourself comfortable and avoid an aching back by standing the item on a support. Working without having to bend also means you'll be less likely to miss any parts.

Ensure good ventilation The safest place to work with chemical stripper is outside in the open air. If you do have to work indoors, open the windows because these products can give off strong fumes.

Stripping lead-based paint Old paint is likely to contain lead. To protect yourself, always wear gloves and a face mask when stripping old paint. Seal the waste in a bag and contact your local council for details of how to dispose of it – don't burn it.

Protect the floor If stripper drips on the floor, it can damage linoleum, vinyl, cork and varnished boards. Spread plenty of newspapers or dustsheets. Stand the feet of chairs and tables in old aluminium baking trays or foil pie cases to catch any runs.

Liquid stripper

A liquid is better for getting into intricate carvings and mouldings but you should take care that it doesn't drip on you.

1 Use an old paintbrush to apply liquid stripper. The paint wrinkles and breaks up about 15 minutes after application. Give the stripper enough time to work – if you try to strip away the paint too soon, it will not come away and another application will be needed. If you leave it too long, it will dry and begin to harden again.

2 Remove the paint using a shave hook on moulded surfaces – pulling the tool towards you. On flat surfaces, push a wide scraper away from you. A heavy build-up of paint will need more than one application.

Gel stripper

Use a gel stripper on vertical surfaces. It won't run towards the floor and is more effective. If you don't have a proprietary gel stripper, mix a little wallpaper paste into a water-based liquid one.

1 Protect the surrounding area with newspaper. Apply the stripper in a thick coat, which will slowly set on the surface while the chemicals work beneath.

2 Follow the manufacturer's instructions; it is usually best to cover the paste with cling film and occasionally spray it with water.

3 After the recommended time, scrape away the paste – it will bring the old paint with it.

Caustic dips

A hot caustic soda bath provides the cheapest form of commercial stripping, but also poses the greatest risk to furniture. Items are subjected to a sudden increase in temperature when they go into the dip; then they are hosed with water to remove the chemical from the wood. These sudden stresses cause cracked panels, weakened joints and raised grain. Hardwoods may also become discoloured.

HELPFUL TIPS

• Most chemical strippers have to be rinsed off with water before you apply a new finish, but this tends to raise the grain and make the wood feel fuzzy, so use as little of it as possible. Water can also cause veneers to lift, so use a solvent-based stripper if you are working on veneered furniture.

• If you are trying to strip a piece of furniture that's caked with many layers of old paint, brush on a thick layer of gel or paste stripper and top it with a layer of newspaper. Then fill a garden spray gun with soapy water and use this to keep the paper and stripper wet. Leave the stripper for an hour to do its job. Then lift a corner of the paper to check if the finish has softened. When you can scrape a test area back to bare wood, lift off the paper carefully; you should be able to remove the stripped paint in one go. If the paper breaks up, simply scrape off the layer of stripped paint bit by bit.

• If you're stripping a large piece of furniture, tackle it a section at a time – the top of the table before the legs, for example. By completely stripping one area at a time back to the bare wood, you will feel encouraged to persevere.

• Don't strip a piece of furniture if you suspect it may be valuable. Removing the patina – the surface sheen produced by age – from a valuable antique lowers its worth dramatically.

Tools for stripping

Combination shave hook

Triangular shave hook

Narrow blade paint scraper

STRIPPING

Scrapers/strippers Scrapers or stripping knives have a flat, slightly sprung blade. Shave hooks, with rigid triangular or curved blades set at right angles to the handle, are used to strip paint from moulded woodwork.

Old brushes Don't throw away old paintbrushes; they are ideal for applying paint stripper. Leave the brush soaking in a jar of the stripper for a short time before you need it. Dried-on paint will soon soften and separate from the bristles.

Scourer Use the scouring pad side of a washing-up sponge, dipped in paint stripper, to remove any vestiges of paint and varnish stuck in the grain of the wood. Rub in the direction of the grain.

Wire suede shoe brush (below) This is the ideal tool for removing softened paint and varnish from turnings and mouldings, and for scrubbing it out of open-grained hardwoods such as mahogany and oak.

Finishes

Varnish protects the surface of wooden furniture and enhances its natural colour. Wax and oil finishes are most often used on wood with a natural finish to show off the grain.

Lacquers and varnishes

Lacquer is a popular finish for furniture. It dries rapidly to form a hard, glossy, water-resistant surface. Two-part, or cold-cure, lacquers are fast drying and tougher than cellulose lacquer.

Varnish enhances, protects and seals wood. There are two main types of varnish: acrylic and polyurethane. Acrylic varnishes dry more quickly, so the risk of dust settling on the wet surface is reduced, and the finish stays clear, without any tendency to yellow with age. However, they are not as tough as polyurethane varnishes.

Varnishes are available in glass, satin or matt finishes, either clear or tinted. It is easier to get a good finish with matt or satin varnish than it is with gloss. The latter highlights any surface imperfections, whereas the others hide them. If you want a more glossy finish, you can always apply wax polish over satin varnish.

Preparing the surface

Varnish must be applied to a clean, dry surface. If the old finish is in a good condition, wash the surface with a solution of sugar soap in water, then leave it to dry. If the old finish is worn, strip if off (see pages 118–119).

Fill any cracks with wood filler. Smooth off the wood using medium glasspaper wrapped around a block, working with the grain of the wood. When the surface is smooth, dust it thoroughly.

Applying varnishes and lacquers

Pour the varnish or lacquer into a container. A two-part lacquer won't cure if it reacts with the container it is mixed in, so play safe and use a glass jar rather than anything made of metal or plastic.

1 Stir the varnish or lacquer gently with a clean flat stick before you use it. Do not shake varnish as this creates air bubbles which spoil the finish. Dilute the first coat of varnish with water or white spirit (see page 53, Step 1).

2 Load your brush, then press it against the side of the kettle. This removes any air trapped in the bristles, which can otherwise appear as tiny bubbles on the newly varnished surface. Brush along the grain with smooth strokes.

Two-part and cellulose lacquers allow you little brushing time. Apply them quickly, holding the brush at a shallow angle. Blend in wet edges but don't overbrush, or you risk leaving marks which will remain as the coating dries.

HELPFUL TIPS

• Use a good-quality paintbrush or a special varnishing brush to apply varnish and lacquer. Cheap brushes tend to lose bristles, which stick to the wet surface and are difficult or impossible to remove once the varnish dries.

• Before using a new brush, dip it in a mix of solvent and varnish, and brush it vigorously on a piece of scrap board or paper to get rid of any loose bristles.

• Remove wooden knobs and handles before you varnish or lacquer furniture. Then apply the finish to the knobs and handles separately before refitting them.

Alternatively Use a clean, lint-free cloth to apply the first coat to the wood surface. Apply firm hand pressure to force the sealing coat into the wood – an effect that you can't achieve with a brush.

3 When the varnish or lacquer is dry, sand it down lightly with fine glasspaper, working with the grain, and dust it thoroughly. Then apply further coats. Always apply thin coats of varnish, allowing each to dry overnight and sanding lightly between each coat. Three of four coats of varnish are usually required.

STORING LACQUERS AND VARNISHES

• It is possible to extend the usable life of some two-part lacquers after mixing. Pour the mixture into a clean jar. Seal the top with cling film and an elastic band. Then store in a cool place.
• Invert a tin of varnish for about half an hour after resealing it, then store it the right way up. This will create a better seal and help to stop a skin forming.
• Clean brushes in the appropriate thinners or solvent straight after use. Once the finish hardens on the bristles, the brush won't be usable again.

Oil finishes

Oiling wood
Oiled hardwood is a popular choice for kitchen worktops, because the finish resists moisture and heat well. Make sure that all end grain is well sealed before installation, especially within the cut-out needed for an inset sink. If it is not, water will penetrate it and make the wood swell.

You can also protect timber garden furniture by treating it with oil, rather than applying paint or varnish. Immerse the feet of chair and table legs in shallow containers of oil, so that the end grain can absorb it.

Choosing an oil
Linseed oil is the cheapest of the furniture oils. However, it is not the easiest to apply, takes longer to dry and doesn't give as hard a finish as other oils. If you do use linseed oil, pick the boiled sort, which dries more quickly than the raw product. Thin initial coats with white spirit to speed absorption and shorten the drying time still further.

Danish oil gives an almost clear, durable satin finish and seals the grain. It takes between 4 and 8 hours to dry. It is usual to apply at least two coats.

Applying an oil finish
Oil is the most penetrative of the finishes used for furniture. Because it depends on absorption by the wood, oil cannot be applied over a previously varnished or waxed surface. For instructions on applying an oil finish see page 54.

When coating wooden furniture in oil, you should leave the oil to soak into the wood for about 30 minutes, then wipe off any excess before it turns thick and sticky. If you do leave it too long, apply some more oil, thinned with white spirit to wet the sticky patches, then wipe off.

For a coloured finish, mix a little spirit-based wood stain into the oil before applying it. For a brighter tint, stir in artists' oil colours diluted with a little white spirit.

WARNING

Rags soaked in oil can burst into flames spontaneously as they dry. Drop them into a bucket of water or hang them outside to dry thoroughly before throwing them in the bin.

MAKING YOUR OWN WAX

Traditional recipe

You can make your own wax polish by melting about 500g (1lb) of beeswax. Use the double-pan method: heat some water in a saucepan, then put a smaller metal container for the wax into the hot water. Make sure your kitchen is well ventilated to disperse the inevitable build-up of fumes as you heat the wax.

When the wax has melted, turn off the heat, remove the small pan from the water and slowly add about 300ml ($^1/_2$ pint) of white spirit to the hot wax, stirring all the time.

Use the molten polish as an initial hot wax treatment for bare wood. Work quickly, using a brush to force the hot wax into the grain.

Instant ageing

To make new furniture look older, try making an 'antiquing' wax. Stir a few teaspoons of fine dust from a vacuum cleaner bag into a proprietary wax. Alternatively, add a little black French polish or dark-coloured spirit-based wood stain to the wax.

For mouldings or carved areas, warm your antique wax up using the double-pan method (above), then apply it with a paintbrush and polish it with towelling.

To make a cream wax, add a little water and a dash of washing-up liquid to the wax and shake well. This mixture is suitable for cleaning and restoring waxed and French-polished furniture.

Wax

Traditional waxing involves applying many coats of beeswax and turpentine to the base wood. You can create a waxed finish more quickly by treating the wood with a shellac or cellulose sanding sealer and then using a modern wax polish.

Pick a beeswax polish to which some carnauba wax has been added. This makes the polished surface a little harder than pure beeswax and produces a deeper sheen.

Applying a wax finish

The wood surface must be clean and dry before waxing. Wax polish can be applied over a previously waxed or varnished surfaces as long as it is in good condition.

For instructions on applying a wax finish to wood, see page 55. You can encourage initial coats of wax to penetrate the wood by warming the surface with a hair dryer, immediately after you apply the wax, then rubbing the surface with terry towelling.

Test the waxed surface by drawing your finger across it. If you can see a mark, carry on buffing the surface; if you can't, it's time to stop and admire the shine.

To alter the colour of wax polish, mix a little spirit-based wood stain into it, drop by drop, stirring vigorously, until you have created the colour you require.

Stains and dyes

Stains protect wood and are suitable for outside and inside use. They come in a range of natural tones which imitate different types of timber – from palest pine to darkest mahogany.

Dyes are purely decorative and are for indoor use only; even then they must be covered with varnish, lacquer, French polish or wax. They're transparent; they tint the wood and emphasise the grain.

Dyes are formulated to be absorbed by the wood. They should be used on new, unfinished furniture or thoroughly stripped pieces. If any old finish is left in the pores of the wood, it will prevent uniform absorption. Excess dye will stay on the surface and will be redissolved if a coat of lacquer or varnish is applied over the top. Dried adhesive around joints also prevents dye absorption.

Applying stains and dyes

Wood stains and dyes are difficult to clean off your hands and are almost impossible to remove from clothing. Always wear rubber gloves and old clothes when using them.

1 Strip off any old finish right back to bare
wood (see pages 118–119). Wood stain will
not take on paint or varnish. Also remove
any traces of glue around the joints. Fill all
cracks with a wood filler that will absorb
stain (check the pack). Then lightly sand the
surface until it is smooth.

2 Shake a container of wood stain before
opening it. Pour a little into a saucer. First
test the stain on an inconspicuous part of
the furniture you're working on. Once it's
been applied, it will be impossible to
remove totally, except by sanding the
stained wood down.

3 Dip a sponge or cloth into the stain and
apply liberally and evenly over the surface.
Work in the direction of the grain.

4 Let the area dry before applying a
second coat. If the wood surfaces feels
rough to the touch when the stain has
dried, sand it lightly with fine glasspaper.
Otherwise wipe the area with a clean cloth.
Finish with wax or varnish.

How many coats?

You can emphasise the stain colour by
applying more coats of it to a piece of
furniture. However, the pigments in the
stain will gradually obliterate the grain
patterning, or 'figure', of the wood, as well
as its natural colour.

Traditional French polish

Proprietary French polish is sold in several
different formulations. Standard French
polish is the usual choice for dark
hardwoods, and white polish for very pale
woods. Transparent polish enhances the
grain but leaves the natural colour of the
timber unaltered. Button and garnet polish
produce tones of orange and red-brown,
while adding aniline dyes to French polish
creates a range of bright, non-traditional
polish finishes.

Preparing the wood for polishing

Do not bring a piece of furniture in from a
cold or damp storeroom and start work
straightaway. The wood will need several
hours to acclimatise otherwise tiny bubbles,
caused by air expanding in the wood fibres,
will appear in the finish.

Applying French polish

Apply French polish in a warm dry
atmosphere – about 20°C (68°F) – so that
successive coats dry quickly. If the air is
damp, moisture gets trapped in the polish,
making it turn cloudy.

Open-grained wood will require several
coats of French polish to seal it. Save
yourself time by using a proprietary grain
filler instead, or take the traditional course
and rub a slurry of plaster of Paris filler into
the grain. When the filler has dried, colour
it with linseed oil.

Use an artist's brush to apply French polish to carvings and mouldings, diluting the polish first with a little meths to reduce the likelihood of leaving brush marks. Once the finish has hardened, burnish the high points.

Satin or gloss?

For a high gloss, give the polish seven days to dry hard, then buff with a clean rag dipped in a mixture of meths and baby oil. Alternatively, use metal polish or a proprietary burnishing cream. For a satin finish, rub down with fine-grade wire wool dipped in wax, working in the direction of the grain. When the entire surface is evenly matt, burnish it with a duster.

The rubber method

Always get rid of excess French polish in a rubber – a homemade traditional tool for applying French polish, made from a piece of wadding or ball of cotton wool, covered by a piece cut from an old cotton shirt or sheet – by pressing it hard on a piece of card or scrap wood. The level of saturation is correct when the rubber deposits an even smear of polish.

Using a rubber

Never rest the rubber on the surface, or the meths in the wet polish will start to redissolve the previous coat and leave a blotchy patch. Start a sweeping motion before you bring the rubber into contact with the work and don't stop until you lift it away from the surface. Grip the rubber close to the base of the twist and keep your wrist stiff – movement should come from the elbow and shoulder.

When the rubber begins to run out of polish, squeeze it harder to force more polish out of the wadding towards the surface of the pad.

If the rubber begins to feel tacky and starts to stick slightly to the surface you are working on, the problem is caused by wet polish in the rubber partly dissolving the previous coat. Stop polishing for a moment and flick a drop or two of linseed oil onto the wood, or rub it onto the sole of the rubber.

The brush method

Use the brush-on method to restore polished furniture without having to strip it back to the bare wood. Use fine-grade wire wool dipped in meths to take off the top layer of the finish, rub it down with fine wet-and-dry abrasive paper, used wet, and brush on the polish.

You can achieve excellent results by applying French polish with a brush. To reduce brush marks, either thin ordinary French polish with meths to extend the drying time, or use a brushing polish.

More coats, extra gloss

Dip just the tip of the brush in the polish and apply the first two coats with quick, light strokes – the first one with the grain, the second at 90° to it. This will leave a satin finish on most woods. To progressively increase the gloss, brush on more coats alternately across and with the grain. Remember to clean the brush in meths, not in white spirit, when you have finished work.

SAFETY TIP

Never smoke while using French polish, or work near an open flame, as the solvent in the polish is highly flammable.

A,B

adhesives 77, 82
alcoves
    cupboards 67-69
    shelves 65-67
aluminium oxide paper 48
architraves 78
    putting up/replacing 99-100
    removing 99
balusters
    broken 98-99
    loose 99
bench grinder 16
bench hook 14, 22
biscuit jointer 45
blemishes on wood 112-13
blockboard 18, 19
brackets 61, 62, 64, 65

C

cam lock fittings 71
car body filler 115
chair repairs 117
chest of drawers repairs 117
chipboard 19, 60
chisels 12, 32
choosing and buying wood 17-19
clamps 14
combination square 8, 9, 21
computer desk 76-77
cornices 78
cramps 117
cupboards, built-in 67-69
cutting wood 22-28

D

dado rails 78, 79-80, 84
doors 100-5
    binding (sticking) 101
    dip-stripping 54
    door frame, loose 102
    flush doors 103
    hanging 103-4
    hinges 39, 102
    joints, loose 102
    keyholes 25
    letterplates and knockers 105
    panelled doors 103
    sagging doors 102
    split door panels 100-1
dowel joints 44
dowels 70, 116
drawers
    gaps 117
    kit drawers 74

drills, drilling 10, 11, 29-31
    corded drill 11, 29
    cordless drill 10, 11, 29
    drill bits 10, 11, 16, 29, 30, 31
    drill stand 14, 31
    freehand 30
    tools 11
    twist drill 116

E,F

edge profiles 35
fibreboard 19
finishing tools 13
fixing 39-41
    into walls 40
    metal to wood 39-40
    nailing 37-38
    with screws 39-41
    tools 11-12
    wood to wood 39
fixings 58-59
    flat-pack furniture 70-72, 73
    hollow walls 59
    solid walls 58-59
flat-pack furniture 70-77
    assembly 72-73
    computer desk 76-77
    customising 74-75
    fixings 70-72, 73
    free-standing shelf units 75-76
floor cramp 89
floorboards
    gaps 89
    holes 89
    loose and squeaking 88-89
    re-laying 89
    restoring 89
floors, wooden
    floorboards 88-89
    laminate 94-97
    restoring 90
    sanding and varnishing 90-92
    sub-floors 94
    wood mosaic floor 90, 92-93
frame fixings 58-59
French polish 112
    applying 123-4
    brush-on method 124
    crazed 112
    gloss finish 124
    rubber method 124
    satin finish 124
    scratches and stains 113
furniture
    blemishes 112-13
    finishes 120-4
    flat-pack furniture 70-77
    repairs 114-17
    stripping 118-19

G,H

G-cramps 117
glasspaper 48
glue gun 14
halving joints 42, 45-47
corner halving joints 42, 45-46
cross halving joints 47
tee halving joints 42, 46-47
hammers 11, 37
claw hammer 11, 37
pin hammer 11, 37
hardboard 19
hardwood 18-19, 60, 121
holes, cracks and gouges 114-15
honing guide 13, 15

I,J,K

ink blots 112
joints 42-47
biscuit joints 45
butt joints 42
dowel joints 44
halving joints 42, 45-47
loose joints 102, 116
marking out 43-44
mitre joints 42, 45
mortise joints 47
mortise-and-tenon joints 42
keyholes, cutting 25
knotting 51

L,M

lacquers 112, 120-1
laminate floors 94-97
door openings 96-97
laying 94-97
locking laminate 94-95
round pipes 96
tongue-and-groove laminate 95-96
underlay 94
laser level 63, 79
letterplates 105
Lok joints 70
magic wire 75
mallet 12
man-made boards 18-19
marking gauge 8, 9, 43
measuring and marking 8-9, 20-21
medium-density fibreboard (MDF) 19, 60, 78
mitre box 8, 22
mitre joints 42, 45
mortise gauge 44
mortise joints 47
mortise-and-tenon joints 42

N,O

mouldings 78-83
architraves 78, 99-100
cornices 78
dado rails 78, 79-80
MDF mouldings 78
picture rails 78, 79-80
profile gauge 79
skirting 78, 81-83

nail punch 11, 88
nails, nailing 37-38, 38
annular (ring-shank) nails 38
cut nails 38
masonry nails 58
panel pins 38
plasterboard nails 38
removing nails 116
secret nailing 86-87
wire nails 38
oil finishes 54-55, 112, 121
oilstone 13, 15, 16

P,R

painting 51-52
panel pins 38
parquet see wood mosaic floor
particle board 19
patching wood 115
picture rails 78, 79-80, 84
pincers 11, 12
pipe and wire detector 64
planes 12-13
bench plane 12, 33-34
power planer 12-13, 16, 34
restoring 16
shaping wood 33-34
plasterboard nails 38
plug cutter 115
plumb line 63-64
plywood 18-19, 60
profile gauge 79
rasps 13, 32-33
routers, routing 13, 16, 35-36
bits 36
edge profile 35
guide batten 36
guide fence 36

S

sanders, sanding 13, 48-50
belt sander 49-50
by hand 48, 52
detail sander 50

finishing sander 49
floor sander 90-91
power sanding 48-50
random-orbit sander 13, 49
wood floor 90-91
saws 9-10
circular saw 10, 25-26
coping saw 9, 24
hole saw 9, 25
jigsaw 10, 26-28
mitre saw 9-10
padsaw 10, 24-25
panel saw 10, 22-23
tenon saw 9, 23
see also cutting wood
scorch marks 112
scratches 113
screwdrivers 11, 12
power screwdriver 11, 39, 40-41
screws
countersunk screws 39, 41
fixing with 39-41
types 41
shaping tools 12-13
shaping wood 32-34
with a chisel 32
with a plane 33-34
with a Surform 33
with a wood rasp 32-33
sharpening blades and bits 15-16
shellac filler 115
shelving 60-67
alcoves 65-67
brackets 61, 62, 64, 65
fixed shelves 64-65
flat-pack furniture 75-76
floating shelves 60
free-standing units 75-76
hardwood lipping 62
levelling 63-64
load test 63
reinforced 62-63
utility shelving 61
skirting 78, 81-83
corners 82-83
fixing to hollow wall 83
joining straight lengths 83
mouldings, repairing 83
removing and replacing 81-83
sliding bevel 8, 9, 21
smoothing wood see sanders, sanding
softwood 17-18
spanners 13
spirit level 8, 63
stains and dyes 122-3
stairs
broken/loose balusters 98-99
creaking treads 97
straightedge 8
stripping 118-19
caustic dips 54, 119
chemical strippers 118-19
gel stripper 118

liquid stripper 118
safety 118
tools 119
Surforms 13, 33

T,V

tape measure 8, 20
timberboard (stripwood) 18, 19
tongue-and-groove panelling 84-88
battens 84-85, 87
buying 84
corners 88
lining a wall 86-88
round doors and windows 87
types of board 85
ventilation 84
tool kit 8-14
maintenance 15-16
workbench tools 14
try square 8, 9, 20, 43
varnishes, varnishing 53-54
acrylic varnish 53, 112, 120
applying 120-1
chips and scratches 113
polyurethene varnish 53, 112, 113, 120
tinted varnish 53
wood floor 92
vice 14, 22

W

wall fixings 58-59
wall plugs 58, 59
walls
cutting holes in 24-25
tongue-and-groove panelling 84-88
wax filler 114
wax finishes 54, 55, 112, 113, 122
'antiquing' wax 122
wax polish recipe 122
white ring stains 113
windows 106-9
beads, renewing 109
sash cords, replacing 106-9
wood
blemishes 112-13
choosing and buying 17-19
cutting 22-28
drilling 29-31
measuring and marking 20-21
shaping 32-34
wood fillers 50-51, 54, 114
wood mosaic floor
laying 92-93
repairing 93
restoring 90
woodgrain, filling 51
woodworm 114

Acknowledgments

All images in this book are copyright of the Reader's Digest Association Limited, with the exception of those in the following list.

The position of photographs and illustrations on each page is indicated by letters after the page number: **T** = Top; **B** = Bottom; **L** = Left; **R** = Right; **C** = Centre

50 **BR** GE Fabbri Limited
51 **TL, TR, BL** GE Fabbri Limited
53 **TR, BL, BR** GE Fabbri Limited
54 **TL** GE Fabbri Limited
60 **R** www.CotswoldCo.com
65 **BR** GE Fabbri Limited
66 **TL, BL** GE Fabbri Limited

94 **BL** GE Fabbri Limited
95 **TL, BL, BR** GE Fabbri Limited
96 **CL, BL** GE Fabbri Limited
79 **TR, BR** GE Fabbri Limited
80 **TL, CL, CR, BL** GE Fabbri Limited
99 **BL** GE Fabbri Limited
100 **TL, BL** GE Fabbri Limited

Reader's Digest Basic Home Woodworking Manual is based on material in *Reader's Digest DIY Manual* and *1,001 DIY Hints and Tips*, both published by The Reader's Digest Association Limited, London

First Edition Copyright © 2006
The Reader's Digest Association Limited,
11 Westferry Circus, Canary Wharf,
London E14 4HE
www.readersdigest.co.uk

Editor Caroline Boucher
Art Editor Jane McKenna
Editorial Consultant Mike Lawrence
Proofreader Ron Pankhurst
Indexer Marie Lorimer

Reader's Digest General Books
Editorial Director Julian Browne
Art Director Nick Clark
Managing Editor Alastair Holmes
Head of Book Development Sarah Bloxham
Picture Resource Manager Martin Smith
Pre-press Account Manager Penny Grose
Senior Production Controller Deborah Trott
Product Production Manager Claudette Bramble

The Reader's Digest Association Limited would like to thank the following organisations for the loan of tools, props and other materials for photographic shoots: Draper tools (www.drapertools.com)

Typesetting, illustration and photographic origination
Hardlines Limited, 17 Fenlock Court, Blenheim Office Park, Long Hanborough, Oxford OX29 8LN
Origination Colour Systems Limited, London
Printing and binding Everbest Printing Co Ltd, China

The contents of this book are believed to be accurate at the time of printing. However the publisher accepts no responsibility or liability for any work carried out in the absence of professional advice.

We are committed to both the quality of our products and the service we provide to our customers. We value your comments, so please feel free to contact us on 08705 113366, or via our website at www.readersdigest.co.uk
If you have any comments about the content of our books, email us at gbeditorial@readersdigest.co.uk

ISBN-13: 978 0276 44081 6
ISBN-10: 0 276 44081 1
BOOK CODE: 400-275-01
ORACLE CODE: 250007097H.00.24